IMAGES
of America

Goodfellow Air Force Base

On the Cover: Bombers over San Angelo. High above San Angelo and the branches of the Concho River, student pilots from Goodfellow Air Force Base practice formation flying in the North American TB-25 Mitchell. A medium bomber by trade, the trainer version of the Mitchell served the multi-engine pilot training program at Goodfellow from February 9, 1954, until August 15, 1958, when the last pilot class graduated. (Courtesy of the Angelo State University Library.)

IMAGES
of America

GOODFELLOW AIR FORCE BASE

Dr. John V. Garrett and
CMSgt. Tom Nurre (Ret.)

ARCADIA
PUBLISHING

ISBN 978-1-4671-0434-0

Published by Arcadia Publishing
Charleston, South Carolina

Printed in the United States of America

Library of Congress Control Number: 2019943775

For all general information, please contact Arcadia Publishing:
Telephone 843-853-2070
Fax 843-853-0044
E-mail sales@arcadiapublishing.com
For customer service and orders:
Toll-Free 1-888-313-2665

Visit us on the Internet at www.arcadiapublishing.com

For Judee and Kitty, whose love and support have made all the difference.

Contents

Acknowledgments

The authors wish to thank Shannon Sturm, head of special collections and programs at Angelo State University, and Matthew McDaniel, community news editor of the *San Angelo Standard Times*, for their invaluable assistance in guiding us through their strong collections of images. Dr. Joe Ryan, the 17th Training Wing historian, and Dr. Daniel LeClair, the 71st Flying Training Wing historian, were exceedingly giving of their valuable time and resources, for which they have our eternal gratitude. Armed with her camera, Shelby Kennemer captured perfect images of some of the current exhibits on base for use in this book. Cold War veterans Harlan Bruha, Ronald "JJ" Graham, and Corky Bingham were invaluable in helping the authors better understand intelligence training and base closure, while Pat Potter and Tony Massaro clarified some of the finer aspects of airborne maintenance training. Special thanks go to Terry Casey for sharing photographs from her ever-growing *Goodfellow Then and Now* collection. The authors also wish to thank Larry Tart, author of the multi-volume *Freedom through Vigilance*, for his help in fleshing out several of the photograph captions. Former PAVE PAWS (Precision Acquisition Vehicle Entry Phased Array Warning System) chief of police Robert Krause, and Randy Mankin, editor of the *Eldorado Express*, shared firsthand knowledge of the PAVE PAWS–Southwest beddown and operation, and our good friend Joe Martin remains the go-to expert on all things EC-47. Sculptor Jerry McKenna shared his photographs of Medal of Honor recipient John L. Levitow. CMSgt. Ryan Brown, director, Air Force Enlisted Heritage Research Institute, and Benjamin Jones of the 25th Air Force history office helped the authors develop the professional military education storyline. Tom's son Tom Nurre Jr. provided invaluable writing and editorial assistance. Last but not least, the authors are deeply grateful to their wives, Judee Garrett and Kitty Nurre, for their willingness to read the manuscript for clarity and for their compassion as their husbands struggled late into the night at their computers.

Unless otherwise noted, all images in this volume are US Air Force photographs in the public domain. Other images appear courtesy of the Angelo State University Library (ASU), the *San Angelo Standard Times* (SAST), Shelby Kennemer (SK), and other sources identified within.

INTRODUCTION

The ceremony in front of the headquarters began promptly at 2:30 p.m. on Sunday afternoon, January 26, 1941. It was six days since Franklin Roosevelt took the oath of office as president for an unprecedented third term, having won reelection partly on the promise to keep the country at peace even though the world was very much at war. Six months earlier, on that very spot, native grasses and cactus and a few mesquites still flourished, until construction teams swept in and happily cleared away the brush—happily, because they all had jobs and the Great Depression had not yet truly passed. As the land was cleared the buildings went up, so that by January it had come to look every bit an Army post.

San Angelo was well represented at the ceremony, with more than 1,000 of its citizens in attendance. KGKL, the local radio station, provided live coverage of the event for those who did not attend. Following a short concert by the San Angelo High School band, the city's mayor, W. A. Halamicek, offered some remarks. That seemed appropriate. This was city land, purchased through a special bond election and then leased to the Air Corps at a nominal cost so that the new pilot school would be built there rather than near some other Texas city. San Angelo offered other inducements as well to lure the pilot school, such as utility connections, beacons, an all-important railroad spur, and even some quiet political persuasion.

When the mayor finished, members of the local chapter of the Disabled American Veterans came forward and presented Lt. Col. George Palmer, the post commander, a 10-by-19-foot American flag, said to be the largest in the city. It must have looked incredibly outsized. The flagpole in front of the headquarters was temporary and short. The tall, 72-foot flagpole that would dominate that spot for decades to come would not be erected until autumn. Palmer took the flag and handed it to a three-member flag detail. As a formation of 15 North American BT-14 aircraft on loan from Randolph Field in San Antonio flew overhead, the band struck the first notes of the national anthem, and the flag detail attached the colors. By Army tradition, as the flag ascended and smartly unfurled, the post was now active.

Seventy-five years later to the minute, in front of a new headquarters built on another part of the base, Col. Michael Downs led a reenactment of the original ceremony as the opening act in Goodfellow's *Diamond Jubilee*. There was much to celebrate, not the least being that Goodfellow was still an active base despite some serious brushes with closure in 1947, 1958, 1978, and again in 1991. In his remarks, Colonel Downs, the 43rd commander since Palmer, spoke first to the legacy of those 75 years: "It's Harry Brown at Pearl Harbor," Downs began. "It's Bill Farrow on the Doolittle Raid. It's Stump Carswell struggling to save his crew. . . . That's our legacy." From the moment Lieutenant Colonel Palmer helped raise the colors on this base, "Goodfellow has been integral to the national defense." But Downs also wondered about what Palmer may have been thinking at the moment the colors unfurled. Looking ahead a year, five years, or seventy-five years, what did Palmer imagine for the base? And had he foreseen its next 75 years, what would he have thought?

This is a history of those 75 or so years. It is a history told through the ability of pictures to restore the past, joined to some text to establish a bit of context and make connections. It attempts this in eight chapters. The first five carry the reader forward chronologically, with each chapter organized around a distinct period or era. Thus, chapter one covers the activation of the base, so naturally, it concludes with the original flag-raising ceremony over which Lieutenant Colonel Palmer presided. But it also reviews some of the considerations that brought the base to San Angelo and some of the consequences, good and bad, of building it there. For example, the city's first airport had to close due to its proximity to the new pilot school. Charles Metcalfe, a local landowner, was forced to relinquish part of his property. The city's population doubled within a decade.

Chapter two covers the war years and beyond, because the base stayed open beyond the end of the war, albeit briefly. Here is where the stories of Brown and Farrow fit: in the first two major events involving American airpower in World War II, Goodfellow graduates were there, and in a very big way. All told, Goodfellow produced approximately 10,000 pilots during the war and even established a "Wall of Honor" in one of the cadet buildings to record their heroism. But like so many other installations, it fell victim to postwar demobilization, inactivating in 1947.

Chapter three finds Goodfellow still flying, as defense requirements for the Cold War reactivated it on December 1, 1947. In T-6 Texans painted a garish yellow, Goodfellow conducted single-engine training until 1954, when 90 TB-25 Mitchells arrived for multi-engine training. But jet training was the future, and the Air Force, facing a diminished need for pilots, believed it could conduct that training better elsewhere.

Chapter four begins with Goodfellow's escape from closure, as the Air Force found itself prodded into moving its cryptologic intelligence training mission from March Air Force Base (AFB), California, to Goodfellow. This was the era of Cold War monitoring and the Vietnam War, and the base played a heavy role in training operators for each. It was also, eventually, the era of post-Vietnam drawdown, bringing Goodfellow once more into close contact with closure before emerging in the early 1980s as the designated site for the consolidation of all Air Force intelligence training.

Chapter five begins in 1993, with much going on. First, the 17th Training Wing became the host unit at the base. This was the unit whose heritage included the Doolittle Raid of World War II. Its activation on Goodfellow was a very big deal. Second, Goodfellow not only survived the new and presumably apolitical base realignment and closure process, but also profited from it, as firefighter and seismic sensors training realigned to the base. The third was the terrorist attack of September 11, 2001. The impact on Goodfellow was profound. Within a decade, annual student production had doubled, as the skills Goodfellow produced were very much at the heart of the nation's defense.

The remaining chapters are organized topically. Chapter six addresses special missions, such as the NCO (non-commissioned officer) Academy Goodfellow operated continuously between 1958 and 2008. Also included here is a special mission that launched balloons from Goodfellow's runways between 1954 and 1971 in support of the Atomic Energy Commission, plus the PAVE PAWS radar site that Goodfellow supported at nearby Eldorado Air Station.

Chapters seven and eight are tightly focused. The former reviews the main heritage exhibits on the base, while Chapter eight looks at some special "Goodfellows" not covered in detail elsewhere. That was not the result of oversight; the authors saved them for the end.

One

Building the Airfield

On August 17, 1940, the US Army established the San Angelo Air Corps Advanced Flying Training School. Had Charles Metcalfe walked onto the porch of his beloved Glenmore Manor the next morning and looked east across his ranch to where the Army had just established its school, he could have been forgiven had he failed to notice it. That was because the Army "established" installations on paper. The actual building of bases, the heavy lifting, came later.

In a sense, as this chapter will show, much of the heavy lifting had already been done, by J. Culberson "Bud" Deal and Robert Carr. In 1940, Bud Deal and Bob Carr were members of the San Angelo Board of City Development. Deal was its manager. Carr, a World War I veteran and Air Corps reservist, led the board's Aviation Committee. It was through his Air Corps contacts that Carr learned that the massive buildup of American airpower, then underway as part of the run-up to World War II, would bring with it four new airfields for training pilots. Here was an unmistakable opportunity for city development and a way to support the national defense. Using his Army contacts, Carr arranged a meeting with members of the site committee in San Antonio. Carrying maps and aerial photography of potential landing fields, and armed with a list of good things to say about San Angelo, he and Deal presented their case. At the same time, Houston Harte, a local newspaper publisher, reached out to his close friend "Cactus Jack" Garner, the US vice president, to secure his support. One obstacle remained. Returning to San Angelo, Carr and Deal reported to the board that the Air Corps possessed ample funds for building new pilot schools but not so much for purchasing the land on which to build them. It would boost San Angelo's chances considerably if the city were to provide the land, they said. The board agreed, offering a lease on 640 acres east of the Metcalfe place at $1 per year. The Air Corps accepted the offer. San Angelo had its airfield.

Ready To Fly. It was almost a year before the attack on Pearl Harbor when contractors completed the first 59 buildings and three control towers for the new pilot school opening near San Angelo. Eighty years later, only three of the original buildings remained on base, although a surprisingly large number had found a way to live on in the local community as government-excess additions to houses and schools. The site was selected for its desolation, its flat, forgiving terrain, its fair weather, and its hard caliche base, since there would be no paved runways for another two years. Much of that is visible in this photograph. Taken in late December 1940, it looks north across the airfield and reveals a lone BT-13 Valiant in the foreground, awaiting the arrival of hundreds more aircraft and the start of training.

The First Municipal Airport. Aviation was not new to San Angelo. More than a decade earlier, not long after Charles Lindbergh made his famous solo crossing of the Atlantic, the city council ordered the construction of a municipal airport southeast of the city along San Antonio Highway, across from the future site of Lawnhaven cemetery, as seen above in a 1930 image. The airport's official opening on January 24, 1929, brought civil and military aviation to the city, as student pilots from Kelly and Brooks Fields in San Antonio used the airport as a stopover on cross-country training flights. Taken June 26, 1932, the image below shows an early airshow, with military aircraft lined smartly to the right. (Below, courtesy of ASU.)

Doolittle was Here. Lindbergh never made it to San Angelo, but Jimmy Doolittle did, as seen in this photograph taken October 31, 1931. Although that was as close as he ever got to Goodfellow, Doolittle's connection to the base was established decades later when the 17th Training Wing became host unit on the base (see page 73). (Courtesy of ASU.)

Too Close for Comfort. Looking northwest across the municipal airport in 1936, the future site of Goodfellow Field is visible as flat, open space southeast of the city. The close proximity of the two airfields would prove problematic, however, prompting the city to close the municipal airport in the interest of air-traffic safety just prior to the opening of the Army's new airfield in January 1941.

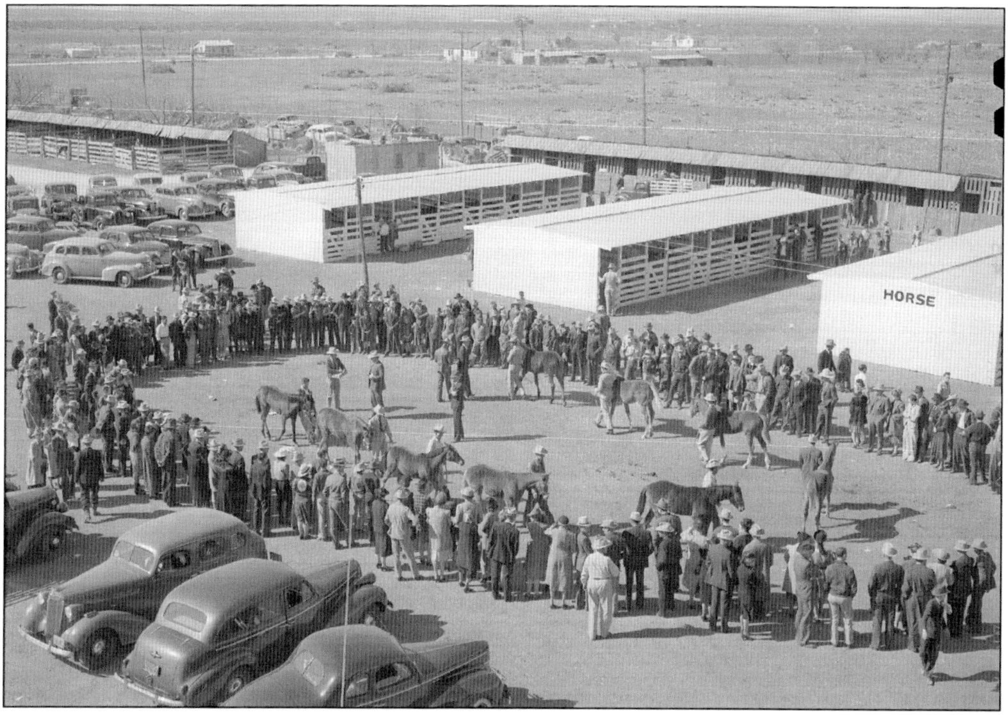

The Fat Stock Show. At the time, San Angelo was small and remote. The 1940 census placed its population at 25,802, but it was perhaps the annual Fat Stock Show, pictured here in March 1940, which best expressed the city's vibrant west Texas character. Part horse and stock show and part rodeo, the gala was the creation of J. Culberson Deal as a way to provide entertainment while promoting better breeding of livestock among local ranchers. A highlight of the event was the horse-judging competition, shown above. Below, the intensity of the rodeo was almost palpable, as seen in the focus of the crowd. As was the fashion, gentlemen wore coats and ties and covered their heads while attending public events. (Both, courtesy of Library of Congress.)

Hitler Takes in Paris. "All you have to do is ask for it," Sen. Henry Cabot Lodge told Gen. Hap Arnold, chief of the Army Air Corps, measuring the mood of Congress as France fell to Hitler. Arnold wanted 54 combat groups, to include 11,000 new aircraft and the pilots to fly them. Annual pilot production had only recently peaked at 246, however, and Arnold's new force would need 7,000 per year. Clearly, new pilot training schools would have to be built. At left, with the Eiffel Tower as a backdrop, Adolf Hitler poses with his favorite artists, architect Albert Speer (left) and sculptor Arno Breker, on June 23, 1940. Pictured below is Hap Arnold sometime after December 21, 1944, when he received his fifth star. (Left, courtesy of Library of Congress.)

DEAL AND CARR. These images show Bud Deal as a young man (right) and his friend, Bob Carr (below), much later in life, standing with his wife, Nona, and Col. Norma Brown after receiving the Air Force Association Citation of Honor for his lifelong contribution to airpower. It was Bud Deal and Bob Carr who led the city's charge in May and June 1940 to convince Army Air Corps officials that San Angelo would make a wonderful location for one of the four new airfields they intended to establish in order to boost the production of military pilots. (Right, courtesy of ASU.)

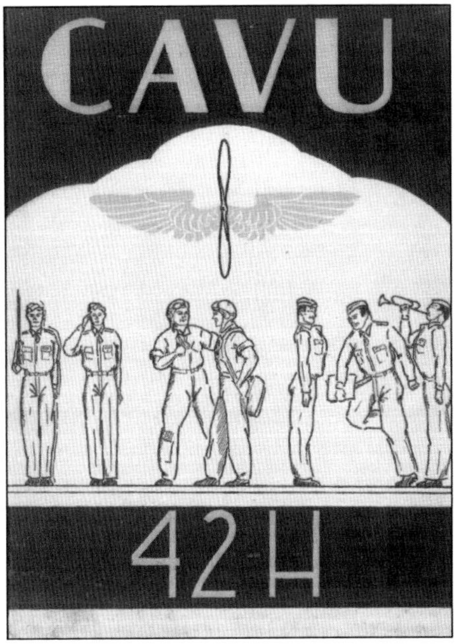

A Wonderful Place to Fly. Pilot classes published class books, much like graduating classes in high schools. Fittingly, Goodfellow's first class titled its book *The Fledgling.* Just as fittingly, those that followed named theirs *CAVU*—ceiling and visibility unlimited—a quality that made flying days many and safe. When considered alongside the flat terrain and the naturally hard, caliche landing surface, it gave Deal and Carr a powerful case.

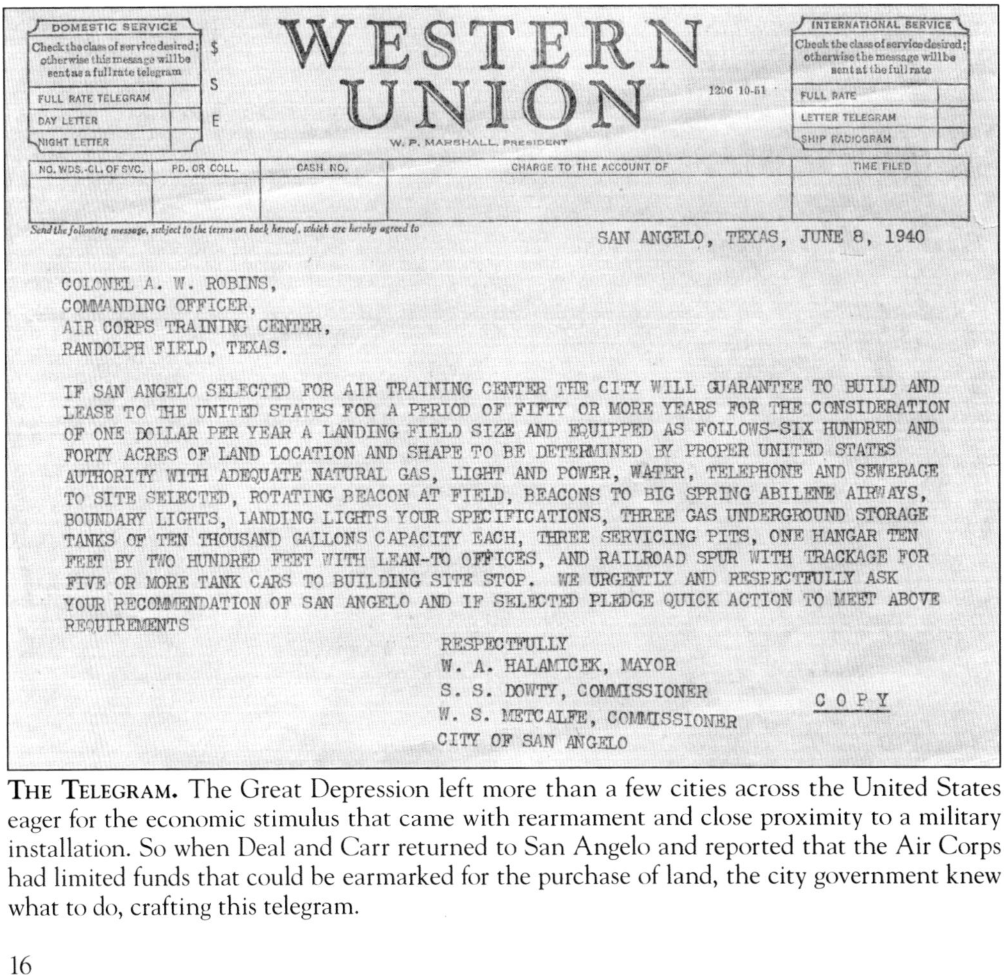

DOMESTIC SERVICE
Check the class of service desired; otherwise this message will be sent as a full rate telegram
FULL RATE TELEGRAM
DAY LETTER
NIGHT LETTER

WESTERN UNION
W. P. MARSHALL, PRESIDENT

1206 10-51

INTERNATIONAL SERVICE
Check the class of service desired; otherwise the message will be sent at the full rate
FULL RATE
LETTER TELEGRAM
SHIP RADIOGRAM

NO. WDS.-CL. OF SVC.	PD. OR COLL.	CASH NO.	CHARGE TO THE ACCOUNT OF	TIME FILED

Send the following message, subject to the terms on back hereof, which are hereby agreed to

SAN ANGELO, TEXAS, JUNE 8, 1940

COLONEL A. W. ROBINS,
COMMANDING OFFICER,
AIR CORPS TRAINING CENTER,
RANDOLPH FIELD, TEXAS.

IF SAN ANGELO SELECTED FOR AIR TRAINING CENTER THE CITY WILL GUARANTEE TO BUILD AND LEASE TO THE UNITED STATES FOR A PERIOD OF FIFTY OR MORE YEARS FOR THE CONSIDERATION OF ONE DOLLAR PER YEAR A LANDING FIELD SIZE AND EQUIPPED AS FOLLOWS-SIX HUNDRED AND FORTY ACRES OF LAND LOCATION AND SHAPE TO BE DETERMINED BY PROPER UNITED STATES AUTHORITY WITH ADEQUATE NATURAL GAS, LIGHT AND POWER, WATER, TELEPHONE AND SEWERAGE TO SITE SELECTED, ROTATING BEACON AT FIELD, BEACONS TO BIG SPRING ABILENE AIRWAYS, BOUNDARY LIGHTS, LANDING LIGHTS YOUR SPECIFICATIONS, THREE GAS UNDERGROUND STORAGE TANKS OF TEN THOUSAND GALLONS CAPACITY EACH, THREE SERVICING PITS, ONE HANGAR TEN FEET BY TWO HUNDRED FEET WITH LEAN-TO OFFICES, AND RAILROAD SPUR WITH TRACKAGE FOR FIVE OR MORE TANK CARS TO BUILDING SITE STOP. WE URGENTLY AND RESPECTFULLY ASK YOUR RECOMMENDATION OF SAN ANGELO AND IF SELECTED PLEDGE QUICK ACTION TO MEET ABOVE REQUIREMENTS

RESPECTFULLY
W. A. HALAMICEK, MAYOR
S. S. DOWTY, COMMISSIONER
W. S. METCALFE, COMMISSIONER
CITY OF SAN ANGELO

C O P Y

The Telegram. The Great Depression left more than a few cities across the United States eager for the economic stimulus that came with rearmament and close proximity to a military installation. So when Deal and Carr returned to San Angelo and reported that the Air Corps had limited funds that could be earmarked for the purchase of land, the city government knew what to do, crafting this telegram.

Houston Harte. Bud Deal later insisted that the telegram had been enough and that no political strings had been pulled. Houston Harte remembered it differently. Publisher of the local newspaper, Harte counted among his close friends the US vice president John "Cactus Jack" Garner of Uvalde, Texas. "It took some doing in Washington to get the site in San Angelo designated," was how Harte explained it afterward. (Courtesy of ASU.)

Signing the Lease. The announcement selecting San Angelo came on June 21. A $300,000 bond sale to finance the offer passed easily one month later. In this image, Mayor W.A. Halamicek and Col. Albert Guidera, soon to be named first commander, take their positions at the table and apply their signatures to the agreement as Deal (far right), and Carr (second from left) look on. (Courtesy of SAST.)

The Railroad Spur. The first work crews arrived on August 13 and immediately set about clearing away the cactus and mesquite. Construction of the promised railroad spur had already been underway for more than a month, so key was it to the timely delivery of building materials. As seen in this 1941 image, the two-mile "Airport Spur" ran alongside the western edge of the airfield before sprouting two additional sidings.

Temporary Construction. The demand for lumber alone was prodigious, as can be seen in this image of a row of barracks being framed in late autumn 1940. Although the contract described this as "temporary" construction good for 20 years, the quality of the materials and workmanship was such that wartime construction still accounted for more than half the buildings on base when Goodfellow celebrated its golden anniversary 50 years later.

Building the Base. Construction began on September 6, with the main contracts for the cantonment and hospital areas going to Hill & Combs. Works Progress Administration funds and labor delivered the lesser projects, such as the water and sewer systems, walkways, parking, and fencing. Pictured here, a row of cadet barracks at the south end of the airfield nears completion.

Dust or Mud. The weather during the first months of construction was for the most part agreeable, until it came time to paint. Choking dust forced road traffic to a halt wherever painting took place. Finally, on November 4, workers welcomed the first rainfall since the project began, only to watch it convert the ubiquitous dust into pooled water and mud, as seen here.

The First Building. The heavy November rains dropped the temperatures as well, moving much of the work indoors until fairer weather returned later in the month. Even so, Hill & Combs reported only slight delays due to weather and on December 9 completed the first building, an officers' quarters along Fort McKavett Road. Colonel Guidera's staff promptly made it a temporary headquarters.

The Reward for Good Work. On January 4, 1941, Hill & Combs completed the first wave of construction, turning over to the government 59 buildings and 3 control towers. The project's chief government engineer, pictured here poring over blueprints for one of the buildings, commended the firm for its "faithfulness and energy," qualities that earned it more work as the contractor for a second wave of construction, set to begin at once. (Courtesy of SAST.)

The Hospital. Also completed on January 4 was the post hospital, a group of 11 buildings interconnected by covered boardwalks. Hill & Combs was awarded the project under separate contract on October 9, 1940, and began construction three days later. The hospital's three wards carried a 111-bed capacity, and additional buildings housed medical personnel, such as the barracks shown here. Visible to the east behind the walkway is the top of a control tower.

Control Tower North. Along the western edge of the aircraft parking apron, Hill & Combs erected three 44-foot high control towers to manage the heavy congestion of air traffic expected when training got underway one month later. The control rooms atop the towers were enclosed in glass and were sensitive, it turned out, to a blinding glare under the west Texas sun, leading ultimately to the addition of outside catwalks.

Sentry Box South. Access to the airfield was restricted by a barbed-wire and cedar "sheep-proof" fence along the perimeter plus two gate shacks positioned inside the western edge of the airfield along Fort McKavett Road. Sentry Box South, pictured here in January 1941, served as the main gate. Driving past the two guards and continuing behind them, a visitor would come immediately upon the flagpole and headquarters.

The Jacobson Gate. Gates became much more elaborate affairs after Sentry Box South was removed from service. Brick walls replaced wooden sheathing, metal roofs replaced asphalt shingles, and costs soared, from $219 for Sentry Box South in 1941 to $76,467 for the new south gate in 1988. In 2006, Goodfellow named its south gate for A1C. Elizabeth Jacobson, a former gate guard, killed during Operation Iraqi Freedom.

Col. George Palmer. Building 910 on Goodfellow is named for George Palmer. Nothing on base is named for Albert Guidera. That was because Guidera became seriously ill in late November, nearly two months before the airfield formally opened, and was replaced as commander by then–lieutenant colonel Palmer. Guidera eventually recovered and lived a long and full life, passing away in 1983 at the age of 91. But it was to Palmer that the honor of activating the airfield and seeing it through its first year of operations fell. Later, Palmer would do the same for the new bombardier school the Army established south of the city in 1942. Below, Col. John Vinay, the wing commander at Goodfellow, and Susan Palmer admire her husband's likeness at the dedication of Palmer Hall in 1973.

First Cadre from Kelly. As a unit, they were not entirely in step, but the arrival of the first 150 soldiers from Kelly Field on January 21, 1941, surely gave the construction crews who built the airfield some satisfaction. An additional 779 troops from Kelly two weeks later fleshed out the 64th Base Squadron and the new 67th and 68th School Squadrons in time for the start of training.

Opening the Field. At 2:30 p.m. on the afternoon of January 26, 1941, Lt. Col. George Palmer stood and saluted as a flag detail raised the colors over the field for the first time. Seventy-five years later, an honor guard team in period Air Corps uniforms presented the colors to a contemporary team in modern Air Force dress, stressing the continuity between past and present as they kicked off Goodfellow's Diamond Jubilee.

Two

Training World War II Pilots

Goodfellow Field's impact in World War II was immediate. When Japan attacked Pearl Harbor on December 7, 1941, the first American pilot to shoot down one of the attackers was a Goodfellow graduate. When the United States retaliated for the attack on Pearl Harbor four months later, a Goodfellow graduate piloted one of the 16 Doolittle Raid bombers. Three Medal of Honor recipients served at Goodfellow during the war. And before going boldly where no man had gone before, Gene Roddenberry trained at Goodfellow.

All told, Goodfellow graduated 10,946 pilots by the end of the war in September 1945. Its training programs were not always successful, however. The washout rate was about 12 percent, slightly lower than the national average. Most failures were for flying deficiency, but a small number were fatalities—28 cadets by the end of the war. It was a risky business.

Goodfellow's impact on the city also was profound. The mix of patriotism and boosterism that drew the pilot school to San Angelo landed a second military airfield in 1942, as the Army Air Forces (AAF) took possession of the nearly completed second municipal airport near Lake Nasworthy and made it a school for bombardiers. Together, Goodfellow and Concho Field, as it was known, propelled much of the city's doubling of the population between 1940 and 1950 (the state average was 20 percent). The economic impact was not measured at the time, but no doubt it was considerable. With growth and prosperity came some discomfort, however. The drone of hundreds of aircraft in the area was incessant. Sexually transmitted disease became a major problem on the two Army posts. And the presence of "courtesy patrols" of military police became an evening fixture downtown.

The end of the war meant a winding down of training. By early 1946, only international students remained. In October, even they left and training ceased entirely. The following May, Goodfellow went on inactive status, leaving a cadre of just a few dozen to manage the sale of surplus property and serve as caretakers for the now silent airfield.

ROOM TO FLY. Three years after the flag went up in front of the headquarters for the first time, this April 1944 image looks east across the airfield to underscore how wonderfully flat the surrounding terrain was for pilot training. The post had grown to nearly 1,000 acres by this point, expanding east by 309 acres in late 1941 and west onto 45 acres of the Metcalfe estate in early 1942. The Metcalfe home can be seen atop a small hill in the far-right foreground. From that vantage, all the markings of a fully functioning airfield were visible. The three control towers built as part of the initial wave of construction had been joined by an equal number of hangars and runways. The parking ramp had been extended and paved and had become crowded with planes. Dominating the main cantonment area were the many rows of barracks, for cadets to the south (right) and for enlisted members near the center. One of these lay apart from the others, however, as Goodfellow would remain racially segregated throughout the war.

The South Hangar. The name suggested additional hangars, but they came later. Completed on April 4, 1941, the steel-framed hangar provided the station's aircraft maintainers 24,000 square feet of much-welcomed indoor storage and workspace. The maintainers belonged to the 92nd Sub-Depot, a tenant unit subordinate to maintenance command. Taxed already by the growing number of aircraft, the sub-depot had the additional mission of training civilian maintainers for other airfields.

The First Class. The 111 members of pilot class 41-E arrived on February 11, 1941, not long after the airfield opened. They came from three of the dozen or so civilian schools across the country that presented the 10-week primary course for the Air Corps. Six days later, flying operations began for the new class. Here, ground crew members and an instructor prepare a BT-14 for an early training flight.

Goodfellow's Doolittle Raider. Anyone standing on the Golden Gate Bridge on the morning of April 2, 1942, might have seen Lt. William Farrow as the aircraft carrier *Hornet* passed beneath. More likely, their attention would have been drawn to the highly unusual sight of 16 dark-green Army bombers chained to the *Hornet's* deck in place of the normal complement of fighters and torpedo planes. Pictured here standing second from left among his crew on the deck of the *Hornet*, Bill Farrow was perhaps the most famous graduate of Goodfellow's first class and pilot of "Bat out of Hell," the last of the 16 B-25 Mitchells to bomb Japan as part of the Doolittle Raid. Completing his mission but forced to bail out over China after running out of fuel, Farrow was captured by Japanese forces and later executed. "Don't let this get you down," the 23-year-old Farrow wrote his mother on the eve of his death, "Just remember that God will make everything right, and that I will see you again in the hereafter."

Pajama Fighter at Pearl. Even before Farrow released his bombs over Japan, a graduate of Goodfellow's second class had already engaged the enemy. Standing second from left in the front row, Cadet Harry Brown is pictured here among members of Class 41-F prior to graduation in May 1941. He was stationed at Wheeler Field, Hawaii, later that year when Japanese forces attacked. Climbing aboard an obsolete P-36 Hawk while clad partially in pajamas, he shot down two of the attackers, scoring perhaps the first air-combat victory by US forces in the war.

Mud on the Apron. When the first classes arrived for training, they found an airfield still very much under construction. In this image, looking south across the apron in May 1941, a recent rainfall has turned the stubborn dust problem into mud, leaving pilots and ground crew to mill about their BT-14 and BT-15 aircraft pondering their predicament. Behind them, control towers center and south flank the new hangar.

GOODFELLOW BOUND. A total of 26 instructor pilots and 48 planes were on hand for the start of training. At first, the planes were North American BT-14 Yales, joined after a few weeks by a handful of Vultee BT-15 Valiants. When these proved challenging for cadets fresh from primary, they were replaced by more modestly-powered BT-13s. Above, a BT-14 is refueled on the ramp at Goodfellow. Below, factory-fresh BT-13 Valiants fly east from the Vultee Aircraft factory near Los Angeles, California, toward Goodfellow. Brightly glistening beneath the rising sun, the yellow and blue paint pattern made the trainers more visible in the crowded skies above the training fields.

Cadet Life. So much was regimented, and so much forbidden, such as being late, or moving in groups fewer than five, or chewing gum outside the barracks or permitting dust inside. Failures in these areas earned demerits, and these earned "tours"—hour-long punishment walks. But finally getting to fly made it all worthwhile, as evidenced by the enthusiasm these four cadets of class 42-H displayed following a morning's flight.

Good(Fellow) Vibrations. The BT-13 was inferior in structural strength and power to the BT-15. Otherwise, the two planes looked the same. They also produced the same effect on windows and on the pilots who flew them, earning each the sobriquet "Vibrator." Eventually, Goodfellow would have hundreds of Valiants on hand, a level of crowding suggested in the drive-by inspection pictured here. (Courtesy of SAST.)

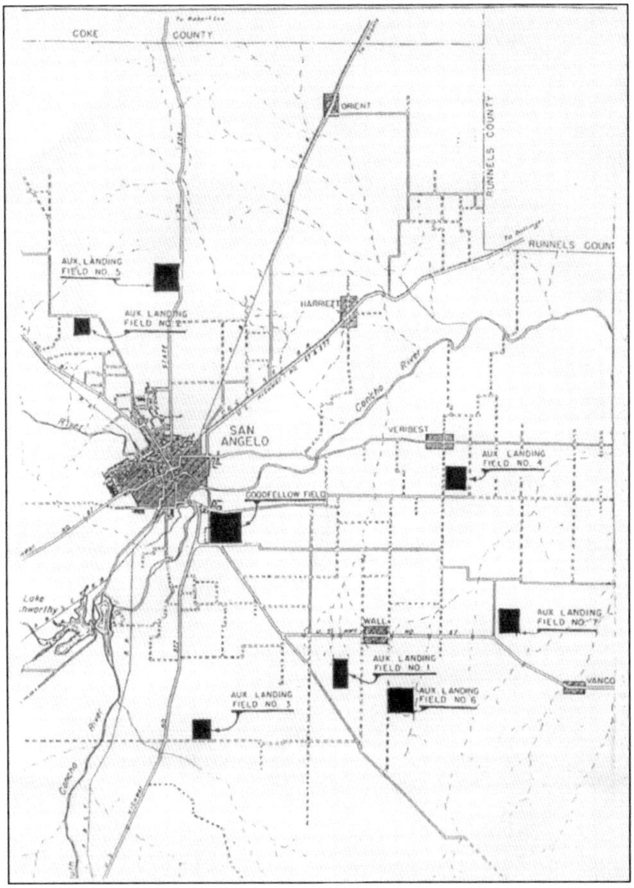

Auxiliary Fields. It quickly became obvious that having so many aircraft sharing the same landing field and airspace severely complicated training schedules and compromised safety. By the beginning of March, base officials found their solution in 202 acres of flat grassland available for lease seven miles to the southeast. Eventually doubling in size, Oates Field was the first of seven auxiliary airfields Goodfellow developed during World War II for practicing approaches and related flight procedures at some safe separation from the main base. Not much more than simple clearings on which an outhouse and a crash shelter or maybe even a cadet shelter could be placed, these auxiliaries nevertheless performed a vital service, accepting as much as 80 percent of the training traffic between sunrise and sunset. Below is auxiliary No. 3, Robbins Field, as it appeared in April 1944.

Seventy Hours. Initially a 10-week program, the basic phase of pilot training was reduced to nine weeks after May 1942 in order to increase production for the war. Flying hours, however, remained firmly set at 70. Pictured here, a cadet and his instructor pan for the camera during an early training flight. The BT-13A in this photograph served as the model for configuring the Valiant on static display at Goodfellow (see page 110).

Formation Flying. The purpose of the basic phase was to make military pilots of the cadets after they had learned the fundamentals of flying in primary. Heavier and faster than the biplanes the students had flown in primary, the Valiants used in basic acquainted students with landing flaps, variable-pitch propellers, and two-way radios, permitting cross-country navigation and more complicated maneuvers, such as the formation flight pictured here.

The First Solo. "It's a most exhilarating feeling—that first solo," Goodfellow cadet (and later Doolittle Raider) Bill Farrow wrote. "Your nerves are taut; you think twice as fast as usual." But then, "tingles race up and down your spine as the wheels make contact and she settles down." Seen here, and perhaps exhilarated, Cadet Reginald Robinson of Class 42-H prepares to solo.

Ground School. While half of the cadets were flying or were on the flight line awaiting a plane, the other half was in ground school learning navigation, meteorology, radio communications, and how to distinguish friendly from not-so-friendly aircraft, preferably at a distance. Never a popular item, Edwin Link's "pilot maker" taught instrument flying while "buzzer practice," perhaps even less well-liked, taught students Morse code, as shown here.

ACCIDENTS. "Safety first" was the watchword at the airfield, and the Link trainer and ground school were ways to limit accidents. Flying was dangerous work. Open any class book from the period, and there is a strong chance of finding it dedicated to one or more classmates who perished in a training accident. Most accidents, though, were lesser mishaps sustained in landing or taxiing, as seen here.

NEW RUNWAYS AND HANGARS. In February 1943, Goodfellow finally added runways. Measuring 150 by 5,000 feet, each of the three runways boasted a 2-inch concrete-asphalt surface over a 12-inch caliche base. At about the same time, the base added a second and third hangar. Both outlived flying operations, as the north hangar eventually became a deployment center and the center hangar, shown here, became a gym.

THE POST CHAPEL. Construction of the chapel began in August 1941 and was completed in November, nearly a year after the airfield opened. There was a reason for that. Before 1941, only 17 Army posts in the United States had chapels. On other posts, religious services were expected to be conducted wherever free space was available. For Goodfellow, that was the recreation center, a 3,663-square-foot facility completed as part of the first wave of construction. All of that changed in spring 1941, when President Roosevelt signed legislation authorizing construction of 604 new chapels within the next half year. Goodfellow's chapel was one of those 604. Pictured above sometime later, it followed the standard Army plan intended as rapid and temporary construction. Below, the recreation center (and temporary chapel) is seen as it appeared upon completion in January 1941.

DEDICATION OF GOODFELLOW FIELD. The airfield's original name was nothing if not unwieldy. An early suggestion would have renamed the San Angelo Air Corps Basic Flying Training School for Bob Carr, in appreciation of all he did to bring the airfield to San Angelo. But Carr declined the honor, and the idea soon surfaced to name it instead for a local war hero. That was the normal approach to naming military installations, and San Angelo had John Goodfellow, a reconnaissance pilot killed in action over France during World War I. The Air Corps approved the change, effective May 27, 1941. At right, John Goodfellow Sr. speaks at the airfield dedication ceremony, held on the Fourth of July. Below, the event in front of the headquarters attracted a large audience from San Angelo. (Below, courtesy of SAST.)

MISSING PORTRAIT. The stage from which John Goodfellow Sr. delivered his remarks featured a large portrait of his son, dressed in the standard Army officer's tunic of World War I. This is the image normally associated with Lieutenant Goodfellow. There is another, shown here hanging above the fireplace at the officers' lounge during World War II. Sadly, the portrait was lost or taken many decades ago and is no longer available for display on base.

BOWLING ALLEY. The completion of the chapel relieved some of the scheduling pressure on the recreation center, making way for the installation of a four-lane bowling alley complete with manual ball-return rails. Pictured here, the commander, George Palmer, recently promoted to colonel, had the honor of attempting the first strike, as members of his staff look on approvingly.

Time on Their Hands. In late June 1944, the first of nearly 600 aircrew trainees arrived. These were pilot candidates, assigned to airfields like Goodfellow to acquire some familiarization with aircraft while awaiting a training slot, an increasingly doubtful prospect as the end of the war neared. Eventually, the trainees were put to work on Goodfellow building a swimming pool, pictured here. The pool later became a detention pond until demolished in favor of a new intelligence training facility.

WAC and Wasp. At first, they were "victims of prejudices," the airfield history reported. Parading on the flightline, this Women's Army Corps (WAC) unit arrived on base in 1943 and remained until 1946. Peak strength never much exceeded 70, but their industry overcame those initial prejudices with what the same history called "acceptance" and "unity." The WACs were housed at the southwest corner of the airfield, where they were joined briefly in 1944 by 18 members of the Women Airforce Service Pilots.

First Peacetime Draftees. On September 16, 1940, President Roosevelt signed into law the first peacetime draft in the history of the United States. Within two months, the first men selected by national lottery entered military service. Not until early 1941, however, did the first draftees arrive at the new airfield in San Angelo, as pictured here at the city train station boarding trucks bound for the base. (Courtesy of SAST.)

The Cadet Club. For cadets who had not collected too many demerits, weekends were "open post," a time to get away and relax after "the strain of the cadet week," as one student put it. For this, members of Class 41-E established the Cadet Club in San Angelo's St. Angelus Hotel, using mezzanine space the hotel's manager generously provided. Pictured here in 1940, the eight-floor hotel was demolished in 1964. (Courtesy of ASU.)

SHENANIGANS. San Angelo supported two airfields during World War II: Goodfellow and the San Angelo Army Air Field bombardier school. Known locally as "Concho Field," the bombardier school is pictured here on VE Day, as airmen digest the news of Germany's surrender. For most of the war, the duty of supplying military police to patrol the city had fallen to Concho Field. With the end of the war in sight, however, Goodfellow took over the duty—but perhaps wished otherwise. In one instance, just before Christmas 1945, the base received a call that a "free for all" involving base personnel was in progress at one of the city's nightclubs. Arriving in their staff car, the MPs entered the building, discovered it to be a false alarm, and exited the club, only to find their staff car missing. They located it two days later, 50 miles southeast of San Angelo and with a flat tire. (Courtesy of SAST.)

Biplanes Come To Goodfellow. In August 1944, biplane trainers such as this Stearman PT-13D began arriving on base, as Goodfellow became the first AAF installation to add primary to its wartime training program. Previously, primary had been the exclusive domain of civilian contract schools. Goodfellow continued to teach basic but replaced its BT-13s with the more powerful AT-6 Texan before ending the basic program following the Japanese surrender in September 1945.

The Stork and the Fledgling. The end of the war and the limited demand for new pilots changed the composition of the classes, as students came increasingly from South America, the Philippines, and Nationalist China. By autumn 1946, even international training stopped; the following May, Goodfellow went on inactive status. All told, Goodfellow trained more than 10,000 pilots for the war, a mission well captured in its distinctive emblem.

Three

Cold War Pilot Training

One of the worries many Europeans entertained after World War II was that the United States would leave the continent and demobilize, as it had after the first war, leaving them alone to face any threat the Soviet Union or its political allies presented. It was a fear that severely complicated American diplomacy, not least because the United States did indeed demobilize, albeit briefly. From a force numbering more than 12 million in 1945, the US military stood at a little more than one-tenth that size two years later. The cuts were especially severe among flying-training units. During the war, the AAF had produced 193,000 pilots; in 1946, only 371 graduated.

For Goodfellow, the postwar cuts came quickly. The basic program graduated its last class in September 1945. Early the next year, a steep programming reduction in American candidates left mainly international students still training at the airfield. On October 8, all training ceased. The following April, Goodfellow received notice of its inactivation, effective May 1, 1947.

It did not last. The Soviet consolidation of power across much of eastern and central Europe and the disquiet that lodged among the western publics and governments inspired on the American side a strategy of containment, resulting in a rapid and unprecedented peacetime buildup of American military power. For the AAF, soon to become a separate service, a new statement of requirements published in June 1947 would increase pilot production to 3,000 annually. As a first step toward achieving that goal, Air Training Command (ATC) reactivated Goodfellow, effective December 1, 1947.

It would take time for the small cadre of caretakers still assigned to Goodfellow to reopen the barracks, supply rooms, mess halls, and office buildings and resume training. Before that, as the Air Force by then had become an independent service, Goodfellow Field became Goodfellow Air Force Base, effective January 13, 1948. Two months later, training resumed for the first of the nearly 7,000 pilots Goodfellow would produce over the coming decade until, once again, it confronted closure.

A Texan over San Angelo. The reactivation of Goodfellow was welcome news to the citizens below, as a T-6 Texan banks steeply over San Angelo. The city first learned of the plans in November, as fresh requirements for an increase in pilot production drove the formal reactivation of the airfield on December 1, 1947. The following month, Goodfellow Field became Goodfellow Air Force Base.

And over Goodfellow. As the same T-6 Texan banks hard over the south end of the north-south runway on Goodfellow in this c. 1950 photograph, the neat, Cartesian features of the base come fully into view. The buildings stood now on government property; in February, the city had deeded the entire site to the Air Force, including the 640 acres originally leased for construction of the base in 1940.

PULLING AWAY. Another pass over the base brings additional features into view as the Texan climbs south, away from the ramp. Appearing against the Texan's retreating tail is the large south hangar, while the center hangar can be seen at the top. Toward the right side of the image, taxiways feed the north-south runway. Tied to the ramp are more Texans—many more.

RAMPING UP. For the selection of aircraft, Goodfellow's basic program picked up where it had left off in September 1945. No longer designated AT-6, the Air Force having dropped the prefixes A, B, and P from its trainer designations, the T-6 challenged students with retractable landing gear and a powerful engine that more closely resembled the performance characteristics of operational aircraft. Above, scores of bright-yellow Texans line Goodfellow's ramp.

GROUND SCHOOL. Before embarking on a night flight, the student would have benefitted from time spent in celestial navigation, as demonstrated above beneath Goodfellow's planetarium in the mid-1950s. Celestial navigation was part of ground school, a major part of the curriculum that focused increasingly on flight safety and attrition. Both were worrying during the postwar single-engine period, as student fatalities climbed to 14 by 1954 and attrition remained stubbornly high, at about 30 percent. All of that changed with the switch to TB-25 multiengine training in 1954. Goodfellow experienced only two further student fatalities while reducing the attrition rate to six percent. Below, multi-engine students take communications training at Goodfellow's ground school.

Night Flight. A student listens to last-minute instructions as he warms up his Texan for a nighttime solo flight. The new integrated basic pilot-training program for Air Training Command combined the former primary and basic phases into a single eight-month program. However, cost considerations and the realignment of the preflight block to Lackland AFB, Texas, shaved two months off the program early in 1949.

Business as Usual. The outbreak of war in Korea in June 1950 drove the US Air Force (USAF) to accelerate pilot production for a proposed 95-wing force. For Goodfellow, production climbed by 37 percent in the first year but then drew back sharply. It was "business as usual," as the local press characterized it. Above, members of Class 49-B pose in front of a T-6. For them, Korean War service was likely.

Officership. "Business as usual" on Goodfellow also included a 235-hour military training track designed to "inculcate" students in the customs, courtesies, administrative practices, and moral responsibilities of Air Force officers. The training program included blocks of instruction on leadership, discipline, Air Force history, basic medical procedures, and a full 78-hour block on ceremonies, inspections, drill, and manual of arms, as demonstrated by these cadets.

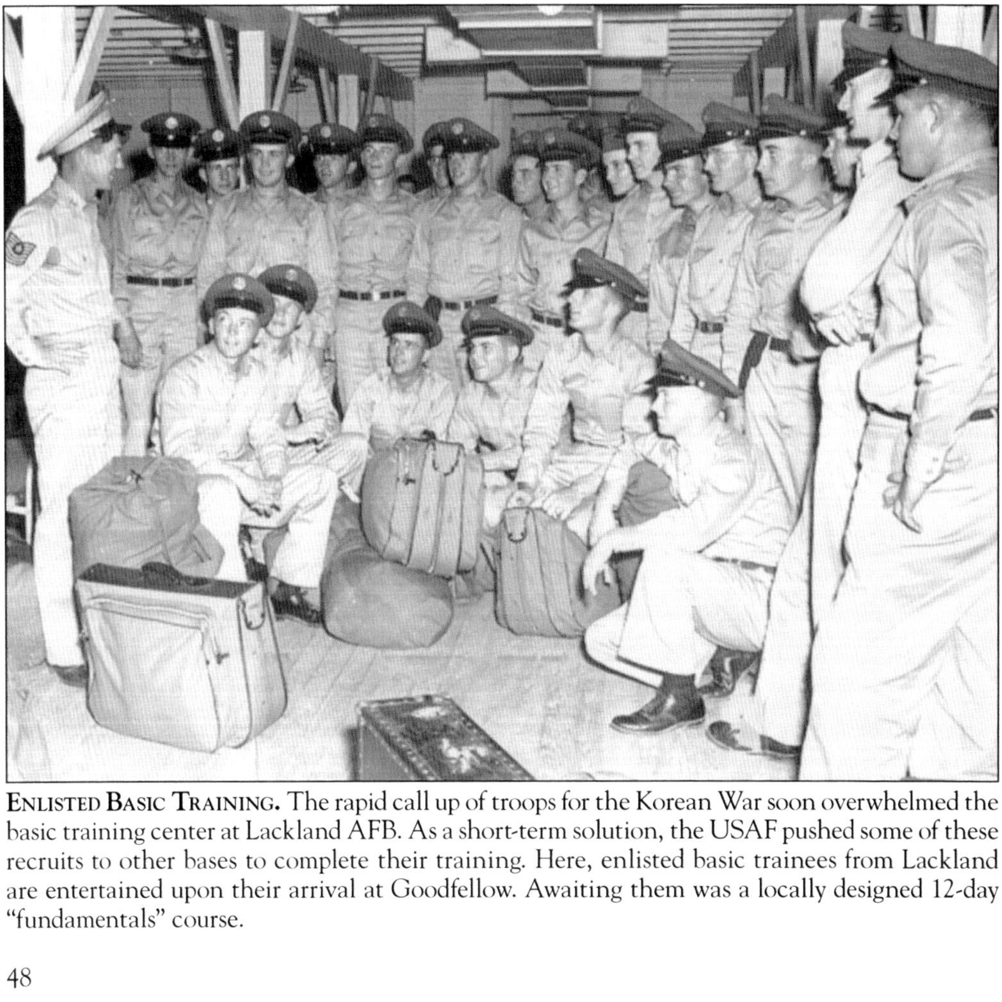

Enlisted Basic Training. The rapid call up of troops for the Korean War soon overwhelmed the basic training center at Lackland AFB. As a short-term solution, the USAF pushed some of these recruits to other bases to complete their training. Here, enlisted basic trainees from Lackland are entertained upon their arrival at Goodfellow. Awaiting them was a locally designed 12-day "fundamentals" course.

Mentoring. As in the previous war, civilian contract schools were called upon during the Korean War to help boost pilot production. Responsibility for maintaining standards at these schools fell to Goodfellow. The base also was responsible for finding a replacement for the trainer these and other schools used in basic, ultimately recommending the YT-34 Mentor, shown here in front of the model it would replace—the T-6 Texan.

Back to Primary. A wing change of command on June 30, 1953, was also an opportunity to celebrate the end of the Korean War three days earlier. By this time, Goodfellow had moved back into the primary business, at least in name. Shocked by the high rate of attrition, ATC had revamped its pilot program late in 1952, instituting a four-phase program in which advanced became basic and basic, primary.

A New Kind of Football. On October 2, 1950, one dozen Dutch students arrived at the base to join class 51-G. The students arrived under the Mutual Defense Assistance Program, an agreement concluded in 1949 among nations of the North Atlantic Treaty Organization. Pictured above in front of a Texan, the dozen Dutch students soon were joined by another 12, followed by students from Denmark, Belgium, France, Italy, Thailand, and the Philippines. Perhaps it was the sight of their American counterparts practicing American football on the base, as seen below, but the Dutch and Danes agreed to demonstrate their version of football at Bobcat Stadium in San Angelo on January 28, 1951. The 2,000 who attended reportedly were "fascinated by the game," the first soccer match ever in the city. The Danes won the match 2-1.

Multi-Engine Training. The end of the Korean War prompted a reevaluation of pilot production goals. As a result of this review, ATC reduced the number attending single-engine school and increased the target for multi-engine training, a re-balancing it achieved by converting Goodfellow from a single- to a multi-engine training base in February 1954. For this, Goodfellow used the North American TB-25, the trainer version of the B-25 Mitchell medium bomber.

A Formation of Mitchells. Student pilots from Goodfellow practice formation flying in their TB-25 Mitchells high above the city of San Angelo, sometime between 1954 and 1958. Visible beneath the lead and middle Mitchells is the white top of the St. Angelus Hotel. The dark bridge just off the right wing of the middle Mitchell is the railroad bridge leading into town, near the San Angelo Convention Center. (Courtesy of ASU.)

The Trojan. For the initial phase of the multi-engine program, students flew the North American T-28 Trojan, pictured here undergoing a pre-flight check. The Trojan was not especially popular. "Everyone felt like a test pilot when he flew the machine," one student at Reese AFB, Texas, complained, as reported in Bruce Ashcroft's *We Wanted Wings*. Within a year, ATC removed all Trojans from the multi-engine programs in order to supply them to the primary schools.

The Wall Dragway. After World War II, Goodfellow's auxiliary fields fell into disuse. With the resumption of training operations, however, the base restored three of these. As increasingly severe drought conditions produced dangerous levels of dust at the auxiliaries, the base responded by paving three 5,000-foot runways at Vancourt auxiliary field south of Wall in November 1953. Years later, the paved diagonal runway became a drag-racing strip. (Courtesy of ASU.)

Wafs on Parade. By December 1944, Goodfellow's WASPs were gone. A little more than a year after that, the Air WACs left. They would return years later, but for a reunion, as pictured above (see image on page 39). Not until 1952, six years after the WACs first left Goodfellow, did the base organization include another women's unit. These were WAFs, Women in the Air Force. The 1948 Women's Armed Services Integration Act had established women as permanent members of each of the armed services, albeit with severely restricted opportunities. Pictured below, members of the 3545 WAF Squadron march in the Armed Forces Day parade in San Angelo in May 1954. The close relationship between Goodfellow and the local community often found expression in the enthusiastic reception the WAF and other base units received as parade participants.

Mitchells on Parade. Years later, anyone standing near this reviewing stand might be tempted to place an order at the Burger King counter. But in the 1950s, this was still the flight line. Looking north, beneath the formations of TB-25s, the center and north hangars are in view. Both later were repurposed and renamed for a couple of Goodfellow's wartime heroes, Stump Carswell and Bob Vance.

The Wing Shield. The WAF squadron pictured on the previous page carried the numeric designation 3545, indicating its subordination to the 3545th Pilot Training Wing. Air Training Command activated the wing at Goodfellow on August 1, 1948, where it remained the host unit until the end of September 1958.

IKE WAS HERE. On January 13, 1957, Dwight Eisenhower became the only US president to visit the base, staying overnight during his inspection of the severe and protracted drought conditions affecting much of the region. Perhaps apocryphally, it has been said that local commanders ordered the parched grass in front of key buildings painted green in advance of his visit! Fortuitously, the rains returned to the region within weeks of his stopover.

JETS. In 1955, ATC disclosed its intention to end all multi-engine training by 1958 and convert to jets, using the Lockheed T-33 T-Bird. Jets had been flying in and out of Goodfellow for several years, and the base soon would have three T-Birds of its own for its transition training program. Above, Col. Alexander Evanof (center), 3545th Pilot Training Group commander, greets the pilot of the first of the three T-birds to arrive, on June 28, 1956.

CLOSURE. The following year, prompted by a drop in pilot quotas, ATC developed plans to close as many as two primary and four basic bases. Originally, Goodfellow was mentioned as a candidate but then dropped from consideration, only to reappear in 1957, owing in part to urban encroachment concerns in relation to jet training. Pictured here is the encroached-upon base as it appeared in 1958.

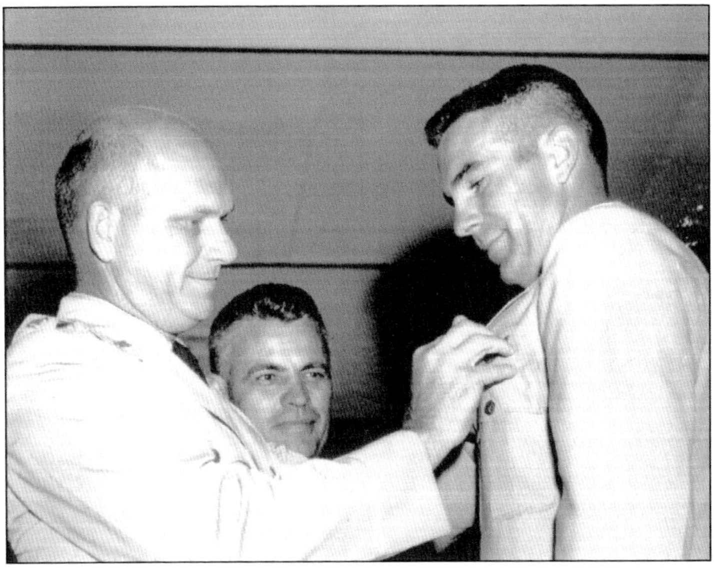

THE LAST GRADUATE. On August 15, 1958, in one of those special moments, former Goodfellow flying cadet G.E. Abernathy, alphabetically the first graduate of the first class, pins wings on the last graduate of the last class, Lt. Charles Wicker, as wing commander Col. Alexander Evanof looks on approvingly. All told, Goodfellow graduated more than 18,000 pilots between February 1941 and August 1958.

Four

Cold War Intelligence Training

In 1956, the secretary of the Air Force, Donald Quarles, visited Goodfellow to help break ground for a pair of brick dormitories. Brick carried a certain sense of permanence that the wood used in the dozens of barracks on base did not. These wooden barracks had been built as "temporary" or emergency wartime construction. The new dormitories, Secretary Quarles stressed, were permanent. Goodfellow, he was there to say, was now a "permanent station."

Within a little more than a year, the base was slated for closure. Secretary Quarles had not deceived; circumstances had changed. By the middle of the 1950s, ATC was transitioning to an all-jet training program. Goodfellow's 5,000-foot long runways were certainly capable of handling jets. Throughout the decade, it had accommodated transient jet traffic and even carried several T-33 T-birds on its inventory. But the training of student pilots in jets benefitted from longer runways. A plan for lengthening Goodfellow's runways by 50 percent was drawn up but soon stalled, as it bumped up against encroachment concerns involving nearby housing.

It may not have mattered. ATC records suggest that budgetary considerations and a decrease in student load by the end of 1957 drove the command to name Goodfellow for closure upon the graduation of its last multi-engine class, programmed for late summer 1958. Much as they had in the past, San Angelo citizens and politicians immediately lobbied the Air Force for a replacement mission to keep the base open. Newspaper magnate Houston Harte and his friend Sen. Lyndon Johnson of Texas, the majority leader, joined in that effort. Eventually, and perhaps not surprisingly, what seemed a perfect replacement mission for the base was identified in the small cryptologic intelligence training school at March AFB, California. Bringing the mission to Goodfellow made a certain amount of sense. The mission was a part of the USAF Security Service (USAFSS), with headquarters at Kelly AFB in nearby San Antonio, so moving the mission to Goodfellow would bring it close to headquarters. But that logic had not stopped USAFSS from moving the mission west to March AFB just two years earlier. In the event, Goodfellow had its replacement mission.

Saving Goodfellow. Houston Harte's personal friendship with Sen. Lyndon Johnson helped get the cryptologic intelligence mission transferred to Goodfellow. As Harte wrote LBJ on April 4, 1958, the day it was revealed that the mission would move to the base, there was "great appreciation expressed for what you did for us." In this 1962 image, LBJ speaks to San Angelo civic leaders.

The USAFSS School. An advance team from the USAFSS School arrived at Goodfellow from March AFB in August 1958 to prepare the realignment. Not long afterward, on October 6, the relocated school opened, featuring intelligence and electronics maintenance training. This c. 1960 image shows the new command emblem on the guard shack at the north gate, with base housing units to the right and the iconic, checkered water tower in the background at center right.

The First Graduates. 1st Lt. Doyle E. Larson, a former enlisted linguist, was acting commandant of the USAFSS School during the transition. Among his key enlisted instructors were MSgts. Ervin C. Fleischman, Lou King, and Anthony P. Reiskis. All were selected for promotion to chief master sergeant when the new E-8 and E-9 supergrades were authorized. Shown here are the first graduates of their traffic analysis training course on January 14, 1959.

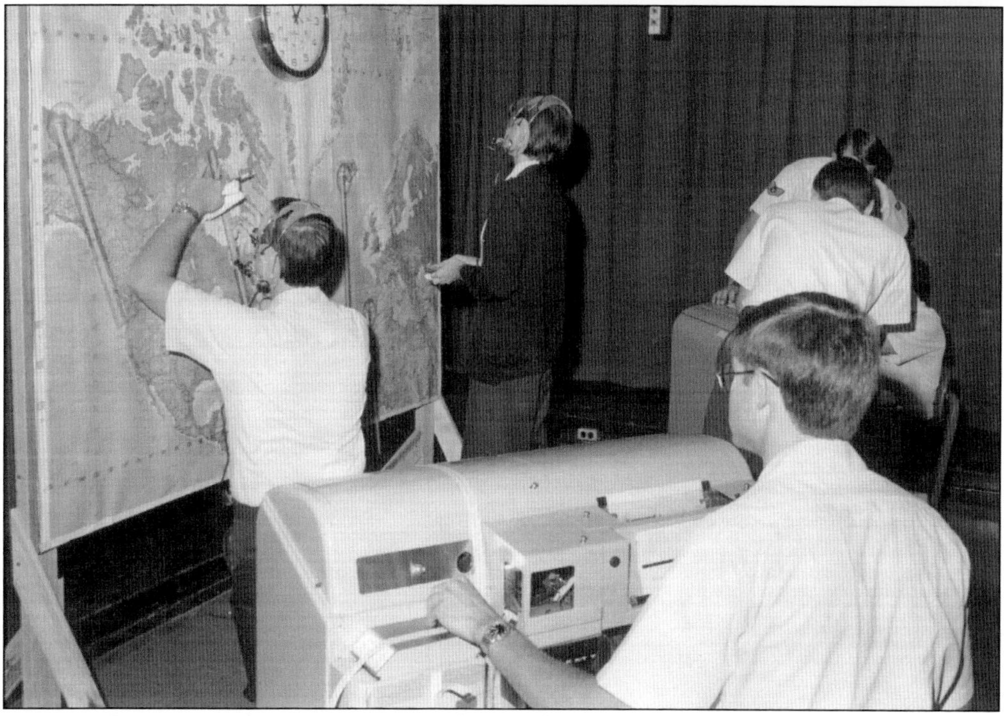

Analyst Course. Students participate in the simulated operations module, the culmination of the six-month communications analyst technical training course. The module replicated the conditions students would see at an operational field site, and enabled them to put into practice the skills they learned earlier in training: security standards, communications analysis, network reconstruction, recognition techniques, orders of battle, flight following, advisory support, reporting methodologies, and teamwork.

Flight Ops Goodfellow. After flying training ceased on Goodfellow, the USAFSS Flight Section at Kelly AFB provided administrative airlift support to the base with two "Bluebird" O-2 Super Skymasters, one of which is pictured here, and three C-118 Liftmasters. Dubbed "Itty Bitty Airlines," they had logged more than 50,000 accident-free flying hours when the operation closed on June 24, 1975. USAFSS chief pilot Col. Grover McMakin earlier had earned his pilot wings at Goodfellow.

C-118 Flight Ops. The Goodfellow C-118s transported VIPs, military passengers, equipment, and classified information couriers. In one mission, Col. John Nikolauk flew the USAFSS commander over the North Pole. Nikolauk later held key command positions at Goodfellow and was the last USAFSS pilot to take off from the base when flying operations ceased in 1975. Here, flight operations personnel pose with the last USAFSS C-118 aircraft on Kelly, on June 24, 1975.

ANTENNAS ON THE FLIGHTLINE. As USAFSS added more overseas operational units with increasingly complex electronic communications intercept systems, the requirement for trained blue-suit maintenance technicians also increased. This C-band Wullenweber QRC-45 antenna was installed on Goodfellow in 1959, probably for maintenance training. It was identical to those used to locate and monitor the communications of Cold War adversaries.

INTERSERVICE TRAINING. Even before relocating from March AFB, the USAFSS School enrolled Navy personnel. The practice continued at Goodfellow until 1962 but then resumed in a much larger way four years later when all services began sending language students to Goodfellow for voice intercept processing training. From left to right, a marine, a soldier, an airman, and a seaman hone cryptologic linguist skills under the watchful eye of their instructor.

And Rivalry. Interservice intelligence training at Goodfellow provided the venue for acting out interservice rivalries, where the annual Army-Navy football game found local expression as a flag-football game. Losing could be humbling, as Army major William Hauser shows in this image from December 16, 1982, as he takes "Staubach," the Navy mascot, for a stroll before presenting the goat to his Navy counterpart, Lt. Raymon Owens. (Courtesy of ASU and SAST.)

Airborne Intercept Trainer. Beginning in 1952, USAFSS operators aboard a lone RB-29 began flying missions in what would later be called the Airborne Communications Reconnaissance Program (ACRP). By 1960, modified C-130 transports had replaced the earlier platforms. Ling-Temco-Vought produced the ACRP systems, and in 1961 installed a prototype operations console at Goodfellow, as shown here. Goodfellow used it as a ground trainer for Air Force airborne intercept operators and maintenance technicians.

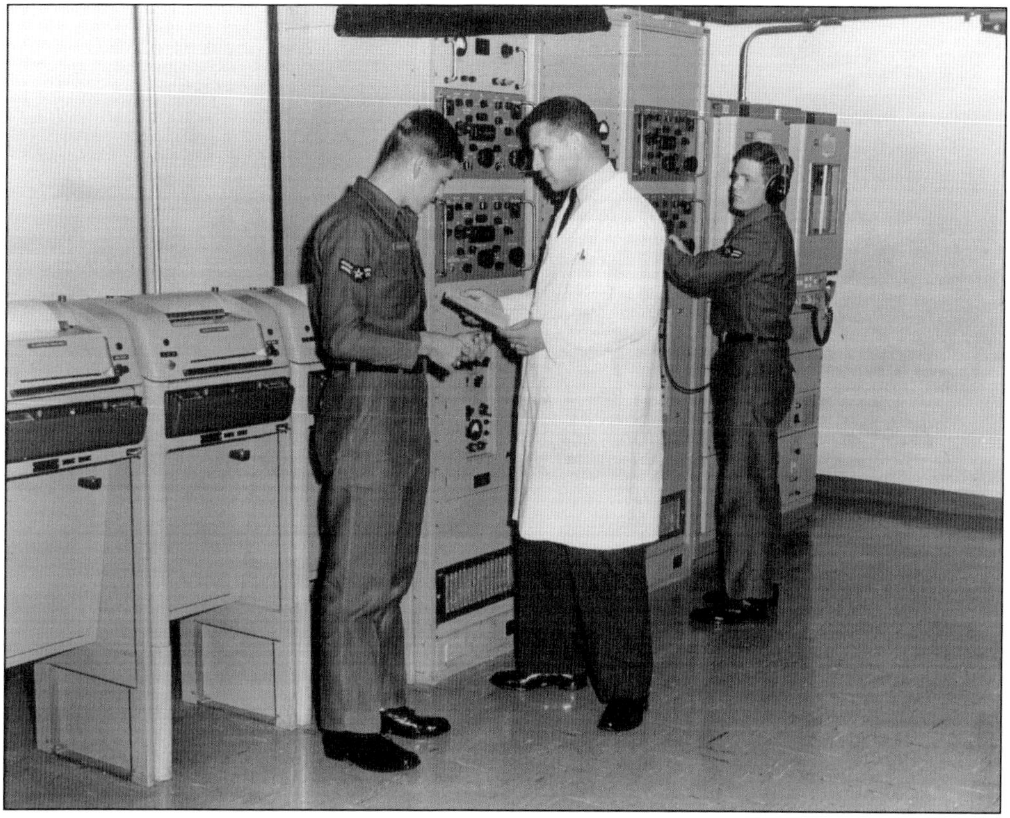

Radio Printer Operator Training. National intelligence agencies routinely monitored the voice, Morse code, and other electronic communications of adversaries. Goodfellow supported this activity in many ways, including non-Morse or radio printer operator training. The training focused mainly on intercepting, identifying, and fine-tuning electronic communications radio signals and printing out the text and numbers traffic on the teletype-like machines, as shown here in the 1960s.

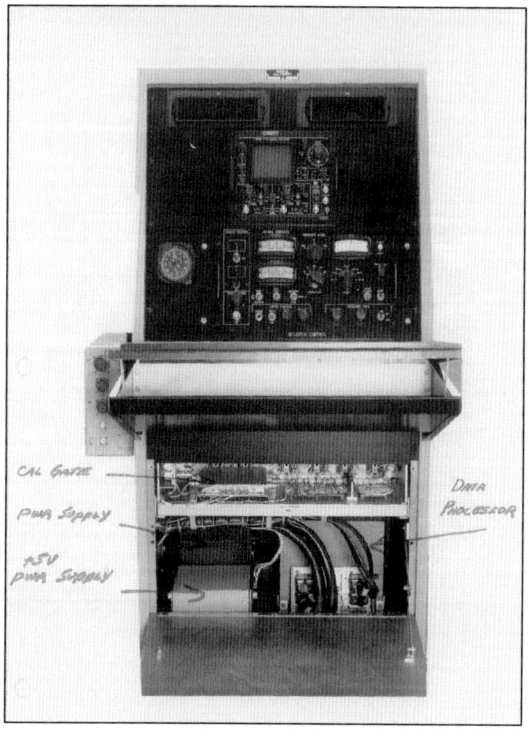

X-Console Trainer. In 1964, the USAF initiated airborne radio direction finding (ARDF) missions over Vietnam using EC-47 aircraft. USAFSS personnel operated and maintained the electronic equipment installed in the cargo bay. Initially, their training was provided in-country by Sanders Associates contractors, but by 1967, Goodfellow had two courses ready. In one, the trainer shown here replicated the "X" operator console—the heart of the ARDF system.

Helmets and Ascots. The 6948th Security Squadron (Mobile) emergency reaction unit activated on Goodfellow July 1, 1963. The "Fighting 48th" had its own operations and support personnel as well as electronics and vehicle maintenance sections. It deployed with towed power units and radio receivers, antennas, communications gear, and area defense concertina wire packed in semi-trailers, deuce-and-a-half ton trucks, and S-141 "Little John" huts. Within hours of arriving at its destination, the unit would set up in the operational configuration shown above in a 1967 "Comfy Bog" exercise photograph. Back at Goodfellow, unit personnel regularly could be seen on the old runways learning to drive and convoy in multiple formations. Members were well known on base for their distinctive helmet, blue ascot, and bloused-boots parade regalia. Led by then-captain Henry Stringer, the squadron executes "eyes-right" in the April 1965 photograph below. The unit relocated to San Antonio in 1973.

ARDF Exhibit. From 1967 until the end of the Vietnam War, Goodfellow trained 6994th Security Squadron ARDF operators, analysts, and communications and maintenance personnel prior to their departing for duty in the war zone. In the foyer of the Norma Brown Building, an award-winning EC-47 ARDF exhibit recalls that history. From left to right, exhibit coordinators John Garrett, Tom Nurre, Joe Martin, and Andy Davenport pose after completing the installation in 2014.

Another Closure Scare. Budget reductions after the Vietnam War triggered an Air Force plan of April 26, 1978, to disestablish the USAFSS and close Goodfellow. As a first step, command of the base reverted to Air Training Command. Meanwhile, sympathetic politicians and local citizens quickly mobilized in opposition to Goodfellow's closure. Here, Sen. John Tower of Texas shares his views during a July 4, 1981, visit to Goodfellow.

A New Wing. On July 1, 1978, ATC activated the new 3480th Technical Training Wing on Goodfellow. Although the base retained the cryptologic intelligence training mission, the USAF School of Applied Cryptologic Sciences (formerly the USAFSS School) was replaced at Goodfellow by the 3480th Technical Training Group. Col. Donald E. Weaver stayed on to command the new wing. Facing away, ATC commander Gen. John Roberts presents Weaver the provisional flag.

Unwelcome News. Turmoil increased as environmental studies and a March 1979 Department of Defense (DoD) training review favored closing Goodfellow. Local columnist Le Kilgore led a protest campaign that garnered hundreds of letters and 20,000 signatures, while the San Angelo mayor wrote a particularly harsh letter to the president. Here, Col. Don Weaver welcomes Gen. Bennie Davis, the new ATC commander, in August 1979. Weaver reassured Davis that he had spoken with the mayor and urged restraint.

ANOTHER ESCAPE FROM CLOSURE. For nearly four years, questions and opinions and study after study about Goodfellow's future dominated the local media. Finally, on October 17, 1981, Sen. John Tower and Congressman Tom Loeffler of Texas brought the welcome news that Goodfellow would stay open and the DoD had designated it the site for Intelligence Training Consolidation (ITC). Additionally, a PAVE PAWS radar had been approved for nearby Schleicher County. (Courtesy of SAST.)

COLLEGE SCOREBOARD

Ark. 42	ACU 28	SMU 28	Baylor 19	Rice 30
Texas 11	ASU 26	Houston.......22	A&M...........17	Tech 23
	TCU 13	SWT...........38	A&I............42	ETSU 42
	Utah State 13	SHSU 14	SFA............10	HPU 0
	Penn St.......41	Pitt 42	Iowa 9	Iowa St. 34
	Syracuse 16	Fla. St.........14	Michigan 7	Missouri 13

Sunday's San Angelo Standard TIMES

110 pages — October 18, 1981 — 50 Cents

Goodfellow to stay open; SAC radar unit coming

'Issue is settled,' Tower announces

John Tower

Bentsen, Loeffler happy with selection

ITC AND GTTC. As part of ITC, Air Training Command activated the Goodfellow Technical Training Center on March 1, 1985. It would be ATC's sixth such training center. Over the next three years, ITC moved advanced imagery, electronic intelligence, targeting, and other general intelligence training courses and equipment from the Lowry, Keesler, and Offutt training centers to Goodfellow. By June 30, 1988, ITC was essentially complete.

IMAGERY ANALYSIS THE OLD-FASHIONED WAY. The Cuban Missile Crisis began when an imagery analyst found evidence of Soviet missile site construction while reviewing film shot from a U-2 reconnaissance aircraft over Cuba. To identify the missile site, the imagery analyst would have pored over a light table much as these students demonstrated three decades later. By then, imagery interpretation was a part of Goodfellow's curriculum, the discipline having come to the base in the late 1980s as part of ITC. For obvious reasons, imagery analysts, or photo interpreters, were known more familiarly as "squints," a name whose meaning would be lost on modern practitioners of the craft. That was because hardcopy film, interpreted on light tables, gave way in the late 1990s to digital softcopy interpreted on computers.

ELINT Training. Realigning from Keesler AFB, Mississippi, the electronic intelligence (ELINT) operations specialist course became the first to begin at Goodfellow under ITC. Here, students learn to operate state-of-the-art receivers to search, locate, and identify ELINT radar and telemetry signals. The Air Force deployed and operated several dozen such systems into the 1990s.

A New Schoolhouse. Col. Charlie Powell and Brig. Gen. Thomas Hickey find some humor as they break ground for building 448 in 1983. Later renamed Brandenburg Hall, the building was the first of six intelligence training facilities constructed over the next decade to house ITC. A fence eventually would surround most of the new facilities, while a pair of brick entry control points and a 44-person security team would control access.

The Old Wing Headquarters. A rare west Texas snowfall blankets the headquarters in this tranquil 1960s image. A part of the original wave of construction, building 158 on Fort Lancaster Avenue served as headquarters from 1941 until 2005, when the new Norma Brown Building on Kearney Boulevard replaced it.

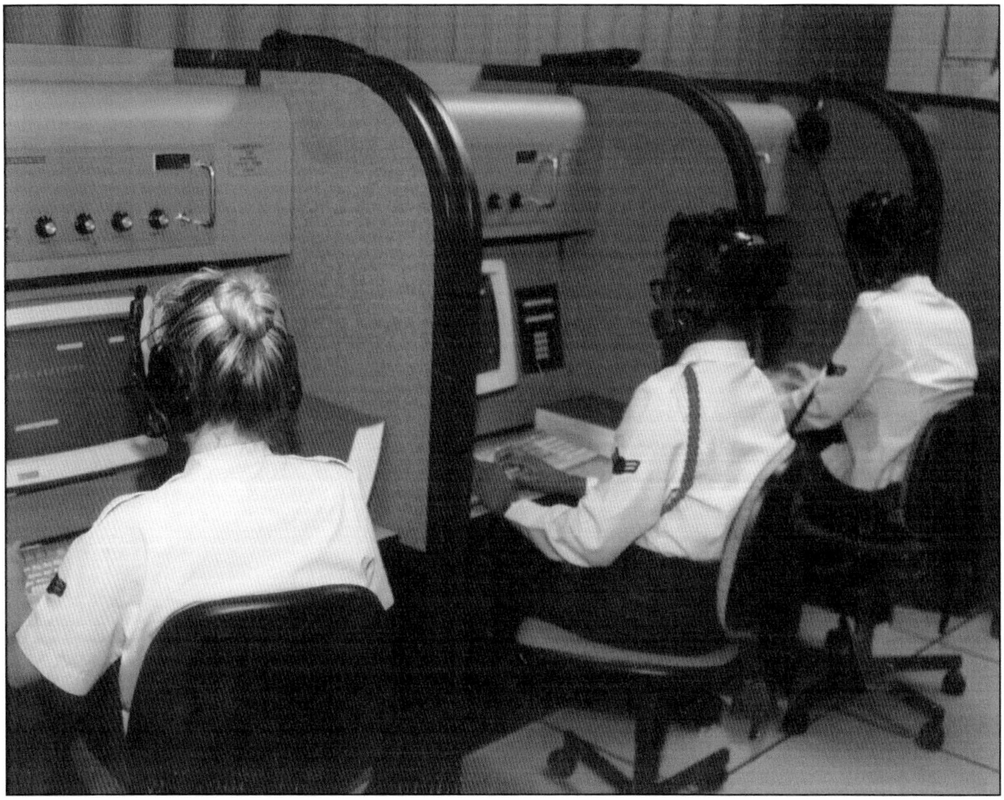

Sentinel Bright and Aspen. Two programs over which Goodfellow eventually held ownership pioneered the application of computer-assisted instruction to intelligence training. Sentinel Bright delivered a two-phase program for cryptologic intelligence training, and Sentinel Aspen, begun at Lowry AFB, did the same for general intelligence training. On January 18, 1988, the first of these programs arrived when cryptologic linguist students began training on the 460-station Voice Processing Training System.

Don't Close Our Base. Goodfellow was not on the initial closure list Defense Secretary Richard Cheney released on April 15, 1991, but Lowry was. While San Angelo's citizens celebrated, Denver politicians protested, eventually persuading the Base Realignment and Closure (BRAC) commission to consider closing Goodfellow as an alternative to shuttering Lowry. Public hearings at San Angelo's 1,500-seat city auditorium on June 18 spilled deep into the surrounding streets, as shown here. (Courtesy of ASU and SAST.)

Still Open. Soon, San Angeloans smiled too. The lively reception Robert Stuart (foreground) and his fellow closure commissioners received from about 3,000 citizens outside city hall on June 18, 1991, made an impact. Two weeks later, the commission submitted its final closure list for the president's signature. Goodfellow was not on it. Instead, Lowry would close, and Goodfellow would receive a piece of Lowry's training mission.

HARBINGERS OF FIRE. In June 1990, two C-130 Hercules aircraft landed on Goodfellow's northeast-southwest runway. In what must have seemed a spectacle, hundreds of base personnel turned out to watch these ordinary aircraft land—on an Air Force base. In fairness, Goodfellow had not had a flying mission for decades. And the arrival of the Hercs was the first tangible evidence that new missions were coming. Above, the two C-130s rest on the runway as a sailor welcomes a superior officer onto the Goodfellow Technical Training Center during Navy Week, October 1991. Standing in front of the first of the Hercs to arrive in the image below is the pilot, Capt. Alan Rees of the Tennessee Air National Guard, and his father, John Rees, a San Angelo resident and former commander of Goodfellow.

Five

Training for the War on Terror

The end of the Cold War left the United States needing fewer military forces. A smaller force required fewer bases to support it and, organizationally, fewer units to hold those reduced numbers. For the Air Force, as it set about eliminating excess bases through the BRAC process and excess wings through inactivations, it quickly became apparent that some of the wings it was standing down had an awful lot of important heritage associated with them. "If we're not careful," Air Force chief of staff Gen. Tony McPeak warned, "We'll whittle away at our legacy, we'll create a new kind of hollow Air Force—one that's lost its heritage, its heroes, its famous campaigns, its core values."

So, the Air Force set about restoring its most distinguished flags by starting at the beginning. "We decided first to preserve our 13 oldest wings," McPeak explained. One of these original 13 was the famous 17th. This was the unit that flew the Doolittle Raid. It was the first US air unit to sink an enemy submarine during World War II and the first to sink subs along both coasts. It was the first to bomb all three Axis countries, and the first to earn the French *croix de guerre avec palme*. Its personnel provided the core cadre for so many World War II bomb groups that it earned the sobriquet "the Daddy of Them All."

This was the kind of heritage General McPeak dared not let perish. So, he pulled the 17th out of retirement and returned it to active duty at Goodfellow on July 1, 1993. The timing was fortuitous. Goodfellow had recently absorbed the general intelligence training mission from across the Air Force. To this, BRAC now added the joint firefighter training mission from Chanute AFB and the much smaller seismic sensors training mission from Lowry AFB. Goodfellow was growing but never more so than in the wake of the terrorist attacks of September 11, 2001. Within a decade, annual graduations from Goodfellow had doubled while the construction of dormitories and other infrastructure surged to keep pace.

ACTIVATION. The activation ceremony took place in the morning. It was already hot. This was west Texas, on the first of July 1993. Worse, the surface of Goodfellow's parade field was black macadam, a legacy of its pilot-training past. Accepting the salute in this image is Col. Joseph Wehrle, the first commander of the 17th Training Wing. Wehrle would retire 10 years later with the rank of lieutenant general.

THE WING COLORS. The lineage of the 17th Training Wing descends from the 17th Bombardment Wing, activated May 10, 1952. Later, to preserve the heritage of inactive World War II air combat groups, the USAF elected to bestow the heritage of those groups on like-numbered postwar wings. That was the path by which the 17th Training Wing inherited the history and displayed the streamers of the famous 17th Bombardment Group.

THE LAST TO LAND. The two Hercs pictured on page 72 were not the last fixed-wing aircraft to land on Goodfellow. On September 17, 1993, an F-15 Eagle touched down on the base, but not under its own power. A CH-47 Chinook helicopter ferried it in and deposited it onto the parking lot behind the old motor pool for use as a rescue trainer in the new fire-training mission. Because construction of the fire academy had been delayed, Goodfellow used the parking lot and nearby classrooms as a workaround solution.

A CHANUTE BURN. When Goodfellow first came under consideration for the firefighter-training mission, base officials wanted to be sure the local community understood what was coming. Scheduling a series of town hall meetings to brief city residents and field questions, the base also arranged a civic-leader tour of Chanute. The plumes of thick black smoke rising from this JP-4 training burn could not have been a welcome sight.

A Goodfellow Burn. Perhaps the most striking feature of the live-fire training burns at Goodfellow was that there was so little smoke. That was due to the fuel. When the burn pits first began operating on Goodfellow in 1996, they burned liquid propane gas plus a small amount of JP-8. Eventually, they burned propane alone, producing what seemed more like steam than smoke, as seen in this c. 2015 training exercise.

Ground Breaking. Either they planned to build the new fire academy inside the officer's club, or it was raining at the site. The event already had been delayed by a DoD construction moratorium plus a petition from Rantoul, Illinois, near Chanute, to keep the fire school in place as a civilian operation. When approval finally arrived, Sen. Phil Gramm (center) led the indoor ground breaking on November 29, 1992. (Courtesy of ASU.)

THE GARLAND ACADEMY. The name over the front entrance declared it a joint facility. Indeed, the Army and Air Force had previously consolidated their training at Chanute, and the Marines joined within months of the school's opening in January 1995 at Goodfellow, followed later by the Navy. In August, the joint school was renamed for CWO Louis F. Garland, known to many as the father of professional military firefighting.

KEEPING IT CLEAN. The live-fire burn pits were used in training for the first time in May 1996. Before that, students graduated with a training deficiency based on lack of live-fire experience. Looking southeast across the new and sprawling Garland Fire Academy, a live-fire event at the large frame aircraft trainer dominates the foreground. Water used in these training fires was captured, cleaned, and recycled for additional training events.

SPINSTRA. Members of the Special Instruments Training program (SPINSTRA) take time to pose for the camera while preparing a seismic device for insertion beneath Goodfellow in 1997. SPINSTRA resided previously at Lowry AFB, where it went by the name seismic sensors before moving to Goodfellow in 1994 and reacquiring its older and more exotic, if less descriptive name. SPINSTRA graduates maintained and operated specialized equipment for monitoring compliance with international nuclear agreements.

The 1995 "Tornado." In May 1953, a severe tornado tore across northern San Angelo, killing 13. Forty-two years later, another struck—perhaps. There remains some dispute whether it was a tornado at all, although there is no denying the destruction. On Goodfellow, roofs were torn from buildings, a C-130 Hercules was carried across a field, and the chapel was so damaged it required cables to tie together the weakened walls.

THE TAYLOR CHAPEL. For visitors to the base, what they remembered best after being away for decades was the chapel. Familiar buildings had come down, and modern buildings had gone up, but the original chapel remained until 2009, when it too came down after 68 years. The new chapel was named for chaplain Maj. Gen. Robert Taylor, a former Air Force chief of chaplains and survivor of the Bataan Death March.

REMOVING THE FENCE. The pace of change seemed to quicken on Goodfellow in the 1990s. Computer-based softcopy imagery analysis replaced bulky light tables. Intelligence officer specializations went away, consolidating first to two disciplines and then to one. But perhaps the most visible sign of change was the removal of the security fence from around the classified training compound in 1996, as a new automated access control system went into operation.

More and Better. The terrorist attack of September 11, 2001, had a profound effect on Goodfellow. Annual production soared, nearly doubling by the start of the next decade. Joined to this was a focused effort to establish graduates as critical thinkers and self-learners and to attune training to the learning patterns of these new generations of students. In this 2014 image, student airmen march back to their dorms after class.

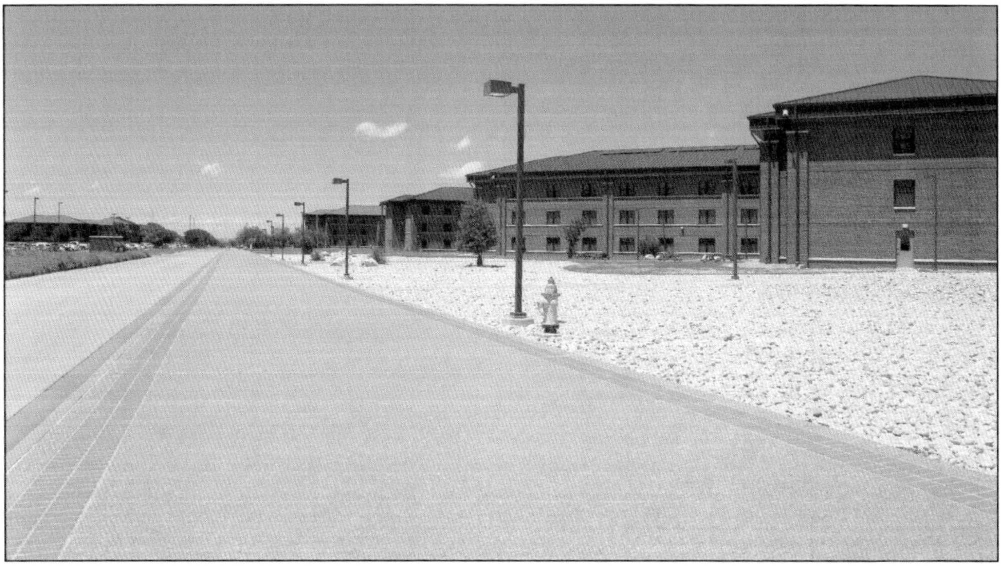

Pipeline Dorms. As student production on Goodfellow soared following the September 11 attacks, it became vital that base operating support kept pace. One area was especially critical: dormitories. The growing ranks of students would need places to stay. By 2019, the number of dormitories built east of Kearney Boulevard presented a striking contrast to the open landing field that had existed there for much of Goodfellow's history. (Courtesy of SK.)

International Intelligence Training. This scene captured perfectly the local community's support for the base and the nation, as Mayor Brenda Gunter of San Angelo (left) and Judge Stephen Floyd of Tom Green County (right) joined 17th Training Wing commander Col. Ricky Mills to cut the ribbon on Goodfellow's new International Intelligence Training Center on November 17, 2017. Repurposing the old NCO Academy building relied heavily on local and state financial support.

Lanham Housing. In the early 1960s, the DoD ordered the demolition of its aging World War II housing projects. One, absorbed by Goodfellow, is shown here under construction in 1941. Because the availability of rental properties, especially for minority members, was tight, Goodfellow escaped the demolition order and retained its under-sized housing. Eventually, the city's donation of 100 acres north of the base delivered additional military family housing to Goodfellow.

Miss Wool and Ewe Little. They are called "animal parades"—ceramic, sometimes fiberglass, statues of animals gaily painted for display in parks or in front of businesses in cities across the world. In Berlin, for example, there are bears; in Chicago, cows; and across San Angelo, sheep—more than three dozen painted fiberglass ovine honoring the region's self-described status as the "Wool and Sheep Capital of the World" and home to the Miss Wool of America beauty pageant. The pageant ran from 1952 through 1972 and Goodfellow supported it, as seen below in 1961. Years later, Goodfellow expressed its support again, unveiling a fiberglass sheep display outside the Jacobson Gate in 2011. Named Lt. Col. Ewe Little, the sheep evokes the memory of Jimmy Doolittle, whose famous raid figures prominently in the heritage of the 17th Training Wing.

Community Support. The local community seemed always ready to support the base in so many ways. Pictured here, the Air Med 1 air-service rescue helicopter and medical team from nearby Shannon Medical Center lands on the base theater parking lot to participate in Goodfellow's Safety Day, May 26, 2005. Approaching the camera is chief flight nurse Judee Garrett. Her son, Jimmy Garrett, stands slightly off-camera to the right.

Chili Cookoff. One of the older base traditions began in 1974 as a way to boost morale, when Cols. Harlan Bruha and John Nickolauk set up a chili cook-off competition in a base hangar. Participation soared, and the annual competition moved to the Goodfellow Recreation Camp along Lake Nasworthy, where it paired years later with a car and bike show. Pictured here, Col. Joe Wehrle leads his colonels in 1994. (Courtesy of ASU.)

Air Force Ball. Goodfellow held its first Air Force Ball in 1977. The annual event originally paired with the holidays in December but eventually moved to September to celebrate Air Force independence as a separate service. One ball tradition joins the oldest and youngest attending airmen to cut the cake, as retired colonel Charlie Powell and Airman Basic Justin Youngblood demonstrate in this 2009 photograph.

Still on Parade. Parading down the streets of San Angelo was a way for Goodfellow to express its pride in service and gratitude for the community's steadfast support. For a number of years, the occasion for this was the annual Armed Forces Day parade. More recently it has been Veterans Day, as in this 2016 image of joint-service members extolling Goodfellow's 75 years of service. Leading the formation is Lt. Col. Jeffrey Sorrell, the 17th Training Wing vice commander.

Six

NCO Academy, Balloons, and Missiles

Goodfellow has always been a training base. During its first two decades of operation, it produced pilots, graduating nearly 20,000 between the arrival of the first class of flying cadets in February 1941 and the graduation of the last class of rated officers from multi-engine school in August 1958. From that moment forward, it trained intelligence operators and maintainers for all the armed services of the United States and select partner nations, graduating more than 330,000 by 2019. Firefighter training arrived as a smaller but vital mission in 1993 after the first round of BRAC transferred the training from Chanute AFB before closing the Illinois facility. One year later, the second round of BRAC moved special instruments training from Lowry AFB near Denver, Colorado, to Goodfellow. Together, the new firefighter and special instruments missions added a further 50,000 graduates to Goodfellow's growing body of alumni.

Although Goodfellow was always in the business of training, it was not always exclusively so. That is to say there were smaller, operational missions to which the base was host. For example, on May 15, 1974, the Department of Transportation established a motor vehicle tire quality grading center on Goodfellow, using portions of former runways as a test track. And for a number of years, Goodfellow's intelligence training mission and the apparatus that supported it also supported a small operational mission, the radio squadron mobile, as chapter four discusses.

This chapter looks at three other missions hosted on Goodfellow. From 1959 to 2008, the base hosted a non-commissioned officer (NCO) academy. From 1954 to 1971, tenant parties on base launched and recovered hundreds of polyethylene balloons in support of an Atomic Energy Commission program to measure radioactivity in the atmosphere. Finally, beginning in 1984, the base supported the operational and, later, caretaker requirements of the PAVE PAWS–Southwest installation near Eldorado, Texas.

THE NCO ACADEMY EMBLEM. Activated in 1959, the USAFSS Non-Commissioned Officer (NCO) Academy operated without an emblem for more than a decade. As finally approved in 1973, the emblem incorporated the academy's instructional focus on world affairs, communication, leadership and management, and military studies. Although renamed the Goodfellow NCO Academy in 1993, it retained its original emblem until it closed on May 28, 2008.

THE FIRST ACADEMY. Pictured here is the first class to graduate the first Security Service NCO academy. The academy was at Royal Air Force (RAF) Kirknewton, Scotland, and its first commandant, according to MSgt. Don Franklin, who furnished this image, was MSgt. Pete Stinus. Franklin is at far left in the second row in this 1956 photograph. Stinus is not pictured. (Courtesy of Don Franklin.)

Academy Signage And History. The April 24, 1952, edition of Air Force Regulation 39-36 formalized the names of the enlisted ranks and the assignment of NCO responsibilities to staff, technical, and master sergeants. The latter two were considered senior NCOs until the Congressional Military Pay Act of 1958 added two supergrades above them, E-8 and E-9, corresponding to the new senior master sergeant and chief master sergeant ranks for the Air Force. Although the academy trained no one in these new top two grades, it nevertheless continued to carry "Senior" in its name until 1963, following the graduation of Class 63-B. In the image above, members of Class 59-C pose in front of the Senior NCO Academy. Below, a member of Class 70-C points out the NCO Academy sign a decade later.

Early Classroom. From its activation in 1959, the early academy operated as a one-room schoolhouse with 24 students per class. The typical 1960s lecture arrangement represented in this image hints at the spartan conditions, with just enough space for student tables, an instructor podium, chalkboard, "butcher paper" flip charts, and a student bulletin board on which individual assignments and subject grades were openly posted. Classroom heating and cooling were notoriously unreliable.

Student Locker Inspections. Students lived in rooms set aside for the academy for the duration of the five-week course. The academy handbook described the proper placement of all items in the two-man rooms. As seen in this 1960s photograph, the laundry bag, military uniforms, and civilian clothes were placed left to right on the hangar bar. Books, headgear, and personal photographs were neatly aligned on the top shelf, also in inspection order.

ACADEMY BEDMAKING. The old barracks attracted spiders, and prevailing winds blew dirt and dust bunnies into every nook and cranny. Even so, room inspections were particularly nitpicky and rarely gig-free. Bedmaking skills were so stressed, some students actually slept on the floor to avoid disturbing their inspection-ready bed covers. Above, CMSgt. John B. Gauthier, the academy commandant, conducts a stand-by inspection in 1963. He expected the bed to be made tight enough to "bounce a quarter," a degree of tension easily imagined in these early images of white-collar (above) and open-air (below) beds. The open-air picture verifies that the service shoes are aligned and fully laced with aglets properly "tucked" inside each shoe. Other footwear had to be clean and serviceable. Students quickly learned to pay attention to even the smallest detail.

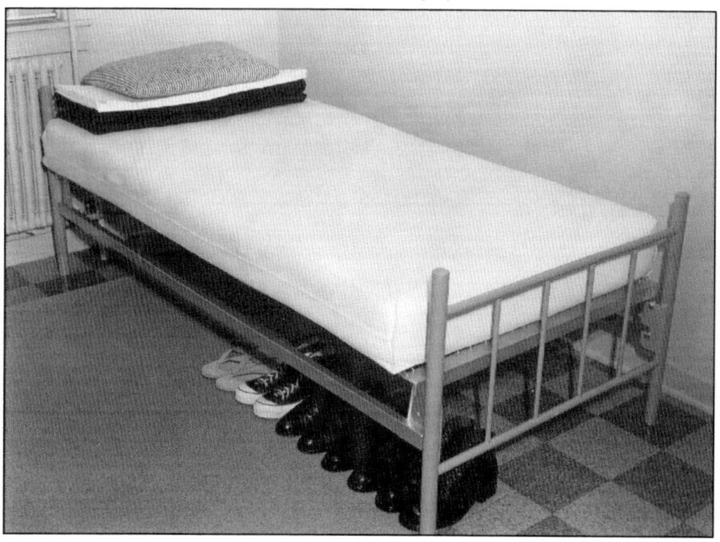

Open Ranks Inspection. Drill and ceremonies were a large part of the academy's military studies curriculum. Students were reacquainted with drill commands they had learned at basic training. By the end of the first day, they were expected to execute the most basic commands: fall in, attention, dress right dress, parade rest, forward march, halt, and fall out. To graduate, students had to master more than 20 commands, including open ranks march, the command given to prepare for this uniform inspection. Initially, "gigs" (such as demerits) were plentiful for such infractions as un-shined shoes, misaligned belt buckles, stray threads protruding from buttonholes or pockets, and overdue haircuts. Students quickly learned teamwork, and self-inspections usually reduced gigs nearly to zero. In this photograph, renowned military studies instructor TSgt. James B. Heath inspects academy class 63-F.

THE MESS HALL. Students studied, drilled, did physical training, and ate their meals together. While at the academy, students wore a colored loop on their shoulder and an academy name tag. The loop was phased out sometime after the Professional Military Education (PME) Graduate Ribbon was established in late 1962. In this image, Class 63-F squad leader, Staff Sergeant Thole (second from left) shares a meal with his classmates.

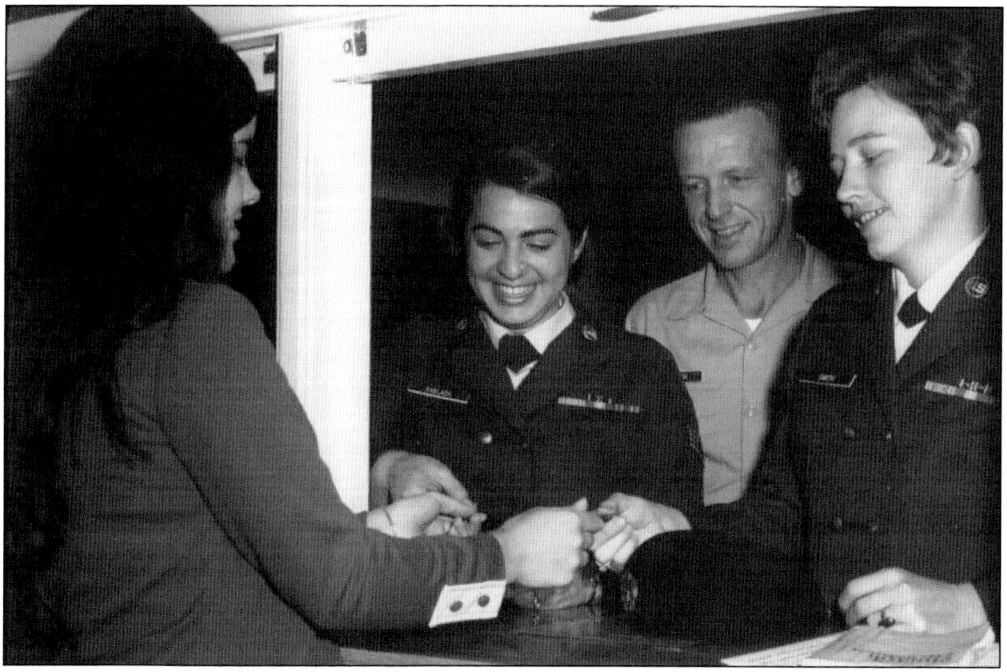

THE ACADEMY GOES COED. Nearly five years before Women in the Air Force were more fully accepted into mainstream job specialties, the USAFSS NCO Academy enrolled its first two female students, in late 1971. SSgts. Millie Sablack and Bobbie Smith from the 6950th Security Group, RAF Chicksands, United Kingdom, are pictured here signing in for Class 71-H. Assisting them is academy instructor SMSgt. James B. Heath.

More Than a Facelift. On August 1, 1979, the Air Force reorganized the USAFSS as the new Electronic Security Command (ESC). The change in name affected the school's name on Goodfellow, of course, but the renamed ESC NCO Academy soon faced more substantive changes. In 1982, stateside academies were directed to share available class seats across command lines. Concurrently, ESC increased the academy's class size to 45 students and instituted a more Socratic, seminar-based methodology in place of the standard lecture format. To accommodate these changes, a $250,000 construction project inside the academy's main facility, building 900, delivered additional classrooms, a learning resource center, a small auditorium, and a highly popular student lounge. Pictured here, ESC commander Maj. Gen. John Marks speaks at the opening of the refurbished facility on April 1, 1985, as Chief Jim Heath and Col. Benton Dishman look on. Colonel Dishman served a number of assignments at Goodfellow, eventually becoming Goodfellow Technical Training Center vice commander before retiring from active duty in 1991.

New Methods. Academy classes accepted non-commissioned officers from across the Air Force. Instructors and students preferred the seminar setting, as it facilitated a fuller exchange of ideas and shared experiences. High standards and academic competition promoted an atmosphere of excellence. Students did their utmost to be a DG—explained facetiously as "Done Graduated" rather than the intended "Distinguished Graduate." Here, academy instructor MSgt. Cindy Willey leads a seminar.

And Technology. Students also welcomed and made heavy use of the resource center computers and software applications that mirrored capabilities at their home stations. They became proficient using the newer technology software to save their notes and papers to take with them back to their duty stations. This image shows NCOA Class 00-6 students using the new robust Zenith 248 computers that replaced earlier Wang models.

NCO PME CONSOLIDATION. The academy staff led Air Force–wide discussions in 1986 and 1987 that resulted in a consolidated enlisted PME program. For the academy, the change drove renovations in building 900 to support a new, five-seminar operation. A classroom in building 901 was remodeled into a modern auditorium, and new staff offices were also added. Each building received a more modern exterior finish, while a pavilion was constructed between them. Above, cutting the ribbon on building 901 on June 17, 1990, are (from left to right) academy commandant CMSgt. Tom Nurre, directors of education and curriculum SMSgts. Gerald Hale and Ed Jones, and ESC commander Maj. Gen. Paul Martin. Below, Dyess AFB representatives present chevrons to Chief Nurre (second from right) for display in the remodeled Dyess Auditorium in building 901.

Student Housing. Class size increased to 80 students following the consolidation of Air Force enlisted PME. To accommodate these larger classes and improve students' quality of life while away from their home stations, the academy commandant negotiated single-occupancy rooms in Goodfellow's new Angelo Inn, the first new construction on the former flightline. There, students now enjoyed access to full laundry and housekeeping services in a hotel-like atmosphere.

Another New Name. The Air Force declared 1992 "the Year of Training" in order to study and implement systemic improvements in enlisted programs. The stateside academies were realigned under Air University, and after November 1993, subordinated to the new College for Enlisted PME. The local name changed again, to the Goodfellow NCO Academy, a name it retained until closing in 2008. Shown here is the academy's building 901.

ACADEMY GRADUATIONS. These were well attended and festive. Commanders and senior NCOs from across command lines had standing invitations. Even after limiting graduates to only two guests, usually a spouse and a supervisor, attendance still swelled to nearly 300 for these mess-dress events. The large crowd and celebratory atmosphere made these joyful and memorable. Graduates clearly appreciated the boisterous support from groups that attended on their behalf as they applauded, banged spoons, sounded air horns, barked like "fire dogs," and whooped and hollered like rodeo fans when the graduate's name was announced. It was an ongoing contest to see who could be loudest. Often, graduates presented "legacy" plaques, proclamations, or other unique gifts to the commandant for display, as in the image above. Below, Maj. Gen. Paul Martin stands with recipients of the distinguished graduate award.

John Levitow Award. The top enlisted PME graduate award is named for John L. Levitow. He received the Medal of Honor for heroism as an AC-47 Spooky gunship loadmaster during the Vietnam War. Although naturally quiet, Levitow frequently presented the award personally at graduations. Pictured here presenting it, Levitow playfully announced, "I present this award in honor of . . . me." (Courtesy of Jerry McKenna.)

Levitow Bust. Levitow visited Goodfellow several times to attend academy graduations. The February 1989 graduation was special, as it marked the academy's 30th anniversary at Goodfellow. It also gave Levitow a chance to view and approve his bronze bust. Pictured here in front of the Medal of Honor display in building 901 are the sculptor, Lt. Col. Jerry McKenna (left), and the commandant, CMSgt. Tom Nurre. (Courtesy of Jerry McKenna.)

Furling the Flag. The reorganization of enlisted PME, begun in the early 1990s, soon led to a drive towards larger and therefore fewer academies. In 2008, the Goodfellow NCO Academy became one of the casualties. Shown here, CMSgt. Edy Agee (right), the 18th and final commandant, furls the academy flag on May 28, 2008. During its half-century of continuous operation, the academy graduated more than 15,000 NCOs.

Heath Hall Memorial. For the Air Force, memorialization is an enduring honor. Long after it ceased operation as an NCO academy, building 900 on Goodfellow remained Heath Hall, named in 1996 in honor of CMSgt. James B. Heath. The ninth academy commandant, Heath was long a fixture at the academy, arriving in 1962 and serving there for 22 of the next 24 years. He died of cancer in May 1996.

Roswell Redux. From 1954 to 1971, Goodfellow released hundreds of polyethylene balloons high into the stratosphere, where they achieved altitudes approaching 135,000 feet. These were the same kind of balloons identified as the remains of alien spacecraft near Roswell, New Mexico, in 1947. Here, a team from Goodfellow inflates a balloon at the San Angelo municipal airport as part of an Armed Forces Day demonstration in May 1962.

Project Skyhook. The Navy managed the lifts from Goodfellow for the first few years, as seen in this early 1954 image of a balloon being readied for launch. Project Skyhook, as the program was called, actually took shape several years earlier, in 1947, when the Office of Naval Research teamed with General Mills to develop a lightweight, low-cost polyethylene balloon capable of lifting scientific research equipment high into the atmosphere. (Courtesy of SAST.)

Lift Off. From the old north-south runway (Apache Trail), often before dawn, mission specialists would inflate and release balloons and their accompanying payload of scientific equipment, as shown in this 1969 photograph. The first payloads measured cosmic rays, but the launches soon fell within an Atomic Energy Commission program to sample the stratosphere for evidence of nuclear detonations. Management also changed, as an Air Force detachment replaced Navy specialists in September 1958.

The Payload. The balloons carried specially designed air-sampling equipment to altitudes within the stratosphere. Some missions, named "Grab Bag," took complete air samples, while others, named "Ash Can," looked for specific nuclear particles or trace gases. Following the balloon launch, aircrews tracked and ultimately recovered the deflated balloon and its payload. This picture shows the relative size of the Grab Bag air sampler compared to the recovery helicopter. (Courtesy of Marc Stevens.)

Recovery. These 1960s images capture the recovery operation. After tracking and locating the payload via radio beacon and visual flight following, the recovery crew is seen above busily compressing the Grab Bag sampled air into gas cylinders. Below, back at the base, the recovered balloon parts are separated for reuse while the air sample cylinders, marked HIV, are unloaded for return to the Atomic Energy Commission for analysis. The Goodfellow balloon activity was a unique flying unit with CH-21, U-6A, C-47, C-130, and Piper Cherokee aircraft. The helicopter seemed especially well suited for the recovery job because of its long landing gear, relatively large cargo compartment, and ability to reach remote locations across west Texas. (Both, courtesy of Marc Stevens.)

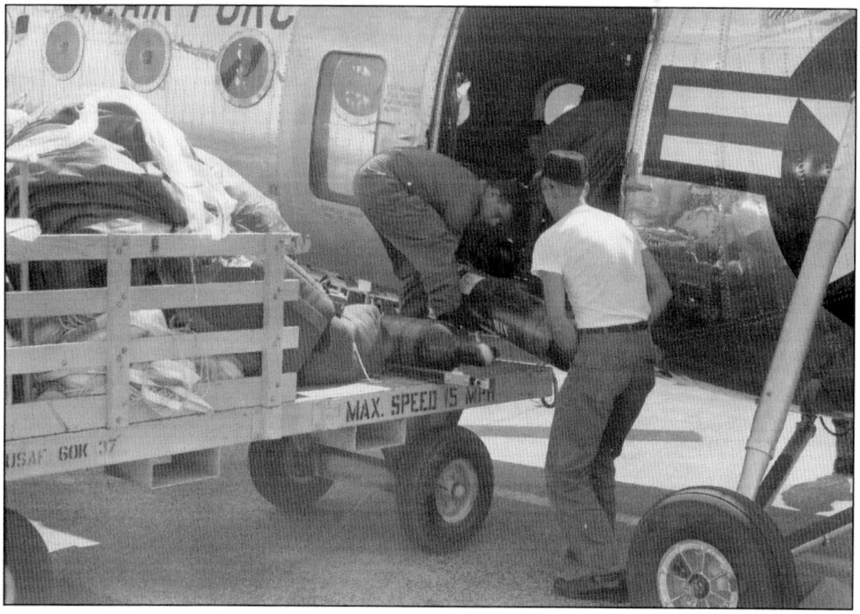

A Wide-Ranging Operation. Although most launches took place on the Goodfellow flight line, the balloon unit also deployed members to launch and recover balloons from other sites in Texas and from as far north as Alaska and South Dakota and as far south as the Canal Zone and Brazil. Pictured here is a CH-21B with its "balloon chasing" aircrew,. From left to right are Capt.Ray Matthews, A2C. Stan Nelson, A2C. James Bowling, and 1Lt. Clark Lovrien. (Courtesy of Stan Nelson.)

Inactivation. The balloon unit on Goodfellow operated under several designations before inactivating on July 31, 1971, as Detachment 31, 6th Weather Wing. Its top-secret "flying sandwich bags" mission to sniff out nuclear particles and trace gases in the fallout from Soviet and Chinese nuclear tests was well disguised at the time as high-altitude weather research. Pictured here is the C-47 flown by "those Goodfellow weather guys" on the morning of its final departure from the base.

PAVE PAWS–Southwest. "There isn't an ICBM around that can sneak past this radar array," Andrew Tarantola wrote in Gizmodo, describing the powerful phased array radar warning system developed by Raytheon Corporation in the 1970s. PAVE PAWS radars beamed powerful electromagnetic pulses to detect and track submarine-launched ballistic missiles. By the early 1980s, the Air Force had sites in Massachusetts and California but wanted additional sites in Georgia and Texas, proposing Mount Susan near Christoval, Texas, as an ideal location. Not everyone agreed. Fearing exposure to radiation and Soviet missiles, local residents rallied at the site in protest, as pictured at right. Eventually, an alternative was found, and the new PAVE PAWS–Southwest (below) found an acceptable location on the Blaylock Ranch near Eldorado, Texas. (Right, courtesy of SAST.)

Rapid Construction. The ground breaking on October 30, 1984, must have seemed like a national holiday with flags, patriotic music, prayers, speeches, and of course, the ceremonial shoveling of dirt. Helping break into their earth were ranch owners Jess and Irene Blaylock plus the commander in chief of the North American Aerospace Defense Command (NORAD), Gen. Robert Herres. The ensuing pace of construction was nothing if not rapid, to which this January 1985 photograph attests. (Courtesy of ASU.)

Goodfellow Support. As wing commander at Goodfellow, Col. Charlie Powell understood the importance of the new PAVE PAWS site not only for protecting the nation from attack but for protecting Goodfellow from closure. The base provided full tenant unit support to PAVE PAWS, including billeting on Goodfellow and transportation to and from the Eldorado site. (Courtesy of SAST.)

Security. An Air Force-trained civilian force safeguarded the facility with special attention to protecting the water supply—vital to keeping the radar cool and operational. They protected the equipment and secured the perimeter with a two-person armed response team, double barrier fencing, infrared cameras, and heat and motion detection systems. This August 4, 2008, photograph shows the empty radar faces, but the fences and deactivated sensors remain in place.

All Systems Go. Air Force Space Command operated the four PAVE PAWS sites. Entirely automated, the systems needed operators only for monitoring, routine maintenance, and final approval on threat warnings. The state-of-the-art computers communicated with each other and with the NORAD Cheyenne Mountain complex near Colorado Springs, Colorado. Shown here, US senator Phil Gramm, Republican of Texas, receives a tutorial at one of the monitors.

Fitting In. PAVE PAWS personnel and Eldorado residents worked well together, especially fire departments who collaborated to control range fires fanned by the relentless west Texas winds. And they played well together too, competing in the annual World Championship Cowboy Campfire Cook-off. As the *Eldorado Success* newspaper reports here, competition for the most authentic chuckwagon was especially fierce, and honors could even be awarded to the PAVE PAWS Rustlers. (Courtesy of the *Eldorado Success*.)

Eldorado Moves to Alaska. Eight years after going operational, on June 30, 1995, PAVE PAWS–Southwest suspended operations, a victim of post–Cold War reductions. The site moved into "warm storage" in August, and its components later were removed to Clear Air Force Station (AFS), Alaska, to be repurposed for the Ballistic Missile Early Warning System, shown here. Goodfellow continued to provide caretaker duties at Eldorado AFS, policing the grounds and performing routine maintenance.

Seven

Planes, Trucks, and Heritage

Goodfellow's rather extensive outdoor display of military aircraft and firefighting vehicles has been assembled mindfully, with a singular focus on the training missions that operated or continue to operate on the base. So, for example, the TB-25 Mitchell that greets arrivals through the main gate represents the scores of Mitchell trainers that crowded the ramp on Goodfellow in the 1950s. Similarly, Goodfellow's T-6 Texan, BT-13 Valiant, and T-28 Trojan represent trainers used at the base before its pilot-training program graduated its last pilot in 1958. Other aircraft displays speak to Goodfellow's ongoing intelligence, surveillance, and reconnaissance (ISR) training mission. Here, for example, is an RF-4C that shot the kind of film on which Goodfellow's imagery analysts once trained, while the RQ-1K Predator and RQ-4 Global Hawk exhibits move forward in time to the ongoing training of geospatial intelligence and other ISR professionals on the base. Equally, the EC-47 Electric Goon aircraft in front of the Norma Brown Building, the wing headquarters, honors the hundreds of intelligence specialists the base trained and presented for airborne radio direction finding operations during the Vietnam War. On the east side of the base, an H-43 Husky helicopter joins an extensive exhibit of 19 antique fire trucks in tribute to the tens of thousands of military firefighters Goodfellow has produced since 1993.

There are other exhibits on base, even if that is perhaps not their primary purpose. There is a pair of Soviet-era MiG aircraft and a surface-to-air missile system. Nestled among the antique fire trucks is a fallen military firefighter memorial. A POW/MIA memorial honors Air Force Medal of Honor recipients. There is a ceramic sheep. Not least, there are two concrete pillars that predate the base but remain on its premises due to a "gentleman's agreement" that, even if not true, has stood steadfastly in their defense.

The Texan. Among Goodfellow's collection of vintage vehicles, three exhibits come together at the wing headquarters to recall the main lines of training conducted at the base. Representing the oldest mission is the newest of the vehicles, a T-6G Texan, configured as it would have appeared in the early 1950s at Goodfellow. The base operated hundreds of Texans from 1944 to 1946 and again from 1948 to 1954. (Courtesy of SK.)

Electric Goon. South of the Texan, an EC-47 aircraft honors the ISR mission that has driven Goodfellow's training focus since 1958. The base trained hundreds of intelligence operators and maintainers for ARDF missions aboard these aircraft, and six buildings on base are named for backenders lost in service. The aircraft on display is actually a C-47A restored as the EC-47Q that flew the final USAF ARDF mission of the Vietnam War. (Courtesy of SK.)

Vintage Fire Trucks. Across the street from the Texan and Goon, a pair of vintage fire trucks honor Goodfellow's youngest mission, the training of military firefighters. The trucks, a 1941 Ford and a 1942 Mack, speak to the heritage of military firefighting. Their location also conveniently marks the turn for drivers seeking the base fire department and, farther along, the Garland Fire Academy. (Courtesy of SK.)

Charlie's Angel. Two aircraft guard the gates. At the Jacobson (south) Gate, a TB-25N Mitchell of the type operated on Goodfellow from 1954 to 1958 for its multi-engine training program stands as perhaps the most iconic image of the base. For years, it bore the placard "Charlie's Angel" in recognition of the role former wing commander Col. Charlie Powell played in retrieving and restoring the aircraft to its former splendor. (Courtesy of SK.)

Zweibrückener. Guarding the north gate from atop its pedestal along Kearney Boulevard is an RF-4C Phantom II. McDonnell Douglas produced 499 RF-4Cs for the Air Force, which dropped it from its inventory shortly after the Persian Gulf War. Goodfellow's RF-4C came to the base from Bergstrom AFB, Texas, in 1990, but its markings later were changed to reflect its far longer service at Zweibrücken Air Base, Federal Republic of Germany. (Courtesy of SK.)

Valiant "Vibrator." Nearly alone at the airpark along Fort Lancaster Avenue, the BT-13A Valiant exhibit came to the base in 1993 as a reminder of the time when Goodfellow operated hundreds. Called "the Vibrator" by the cadets who flew it, the Valiant dominated the basic phase of pilot training during World War II, finally to be replaced by the AT-6 Texan at Goodfellow and other basic schools in 1944. (Courtesy of SK.)

A Trojan from Reese. Base closure has favored Goodfellow, sending it firefighter training from Chanute, special instruments training from Lowry, and a T-28A Trojan from Reese AFB near Lubbock, Texas. Arriving in 1998, the Trojan joined the Valiant on exhibit at Goodfellow's airpark. Unlike the Valiant, however, the Trojan served Goodfellow only briefly and in far smaller numbers, departing the base in February 1955 after two years' service. (Courtesy of SK.)

The POW/MIA/Medal of Honor Memorial. At the south end of the airpark, a black granite memorial records the names of the 61 airmen who received the Medal of Honor. Five served at Goodfellow and are discussed in the next chapter. The memorial also honors all who have been prisoners of war or remain missing or unaccounted for. Dedicated in 1999, the memorial for many years was the scene of 24-hour vigils of remembrance. (Courtesy of SK.)

PREDATOR. Sitting atop a small mound opposite the parade field, Goodfellow's RQ-1K Predator is one of two remotely piloted aircraft (RPA), or drones, on display at the base. It entered the Air Force inventory as a pre-production model in 1997 and was used in Operation Allied Force over Kosovo in 1999. Goodfellow's Predator went on display 10 years later as the nation's first outdoor exhibit of an RQ-1. (Courtesy of SK.)

GLOBAL HAWK. Farther down Kearney Boulevard sits the other RPA. Goodfellow's RQ-4A Global Hawk was one of seven block 10 Global Hawks produced for the Air Force, and logged 4,830 hours during 285 missions, mainly in support of Operation Enduring Freedom. On display since 2012, its location near the ISR schoolhouse makes it a ready showpiece for students training to exploit RPA feeds. (Courtesy of SK.)

Two MiGs and a SAM. Using aircraft and related vehicles to enhance training drove an earlier effort to create a "threat display" from which students could draw conclusions about adversaries' capabilities. Only three displays made it to Goodfellow before the project froze in the late 1990s: an SA-4 surface-to-air missile system and associated Pat Hand radar, a MiG-23 Flogger, and a MiG-29 Fulcrum-A, as seen here at the ISR schoolhouse. (Courtesy of SK.)

Pedro. Nestled among Goodfellow's sprawling display of military firefighting vehicles is a lone helicopter, a Kaman H-43B Huskie in standard rescue helicopter configuration. The USAF deployed the Huskie primarily as an aircraft firefighting and rescue platform for use in close proximity to airbases. When used operationally for overland search and rescue during the Vietnam War, it often carried the call sign "Pedro." (Courtesy of SK.)

Fire Truck Exhibit. Along the troopwalk leading to the fire school is the Fallen Military Firefighting Memorial and an extensive exhibit of military firefighting vehicles. Both ensure that students pass through their heritage as they march from their dorms to class. Typical of that heritage is the 1951 Magirus Deutz ladder truck shown here, whose history includes the rescue of 80 children from a burning school in Bitburg, Germany. (Courtesy of SK.)

The Metcalfe Gate. There is a story about these two stone pillars that persists despite the absence of evidence. The pillars supported the original gate leading from Fort McKavett Road west to Charles Metcalfe's house. An identical pair marks the entrance to the house. The story has it that when Goodfellow acquired a tract of Metcalfe's land in 1942, a gentleman's agreement promised to keep the pillars forever in place. (Courtesy of SK.)

Eight

Inimitable People

Somewhere in the neighborhood of 400,000 people graduated from Goodfellow. A smaller but still significant number were assigned there at one time or another in permanent party status. It is difficult to fix these totals precisely, as permanent party personnel may have been assigned multiple times to the base and many students graduated multiple courses at Goodfellow or its geographically separated units. It is even more difficult to select from among this number some who might be called extraordinary or inimitable, as this chapter purports to do.

The previous chapters include a number of folks known to have done something many would find extraordinary. There is Col. Harry Brown, who shot down two Japanese aircraft during the attack on Pearl Harbor and who later in the war became an ace. Or 1Lt. William Farrow, who flew one of 16 Mitchell medium bombers on the Doolittle Raid. Or Capt. Eugene Roddenberry, who created *Star Trek*. And there are others not mentioned in these chapters. There is Col. Joseph Kittinger, who for decades held the record for the highest jump, at nearly 20 miles. Or Gen. Charles Gabriel, a chief of staff of the Air Force. Or Gen. Lori Robinson, the first woman to command a unified combatant command.

The list runs long, making the selection of 10 for inclusion in this chapter at once easy and difficult. That said, the first selection actually was quite obvious. The base is named for him. Five more are obvious too. Each is a recipient of the Medal of Honor—posthumously, for three of the five. The next is a first—the first woman to command an Air Force wing. Another was one of many who trained or served at Goodfellow and who later gave his or her life in the line of duty. Still another represents those who achieved fame in other areas, like Roddenberry. And the last has done more for Goodfellow and for its relationship with the local community than anyone else known to the authors.

Details. A base is named for him, so one might expect the basic details of his life to be known. But in the case of Lieutenant Goodfellow, there has been some confusion. For example, the memorial plaque that lay for decades at the base flagpole named him James J. Goodfellow Jr. But the man to whom he was junior was John James Goodfellow Sr. Like his father, Lieutenant Goodfellow was John; his family called him James, familiarly, to distinguish him from his father. Or take his date of death: the plaque and his burial marker in France put it at September 17, 1918, but his unit recorded it as September 14. Still, these are small points. What looms large is that the service he provided his country cost him his life—and a grateful nation remembers. (Below, courtesy of Elaine Sorrell.)

1Lt. John Goodfellow. The original purpose of fighter planes, or pursuit, as they were called, was to shoot down reconnaissance planes. Reconnaissance spotted for artillery and exposed the enemy and his movements. Lieutenant Goodfellow was a reconnaissance pilot. Infused with Progressive-era idealism and a will to help end all wars, as his letters home suggest, the San Angelo native left the University of Texas after two years because his country went to war. He was there in France on September 12, 1918, flying his first mission as a part of his country's first offensive, near St. Mihiel. His mission the next day was scratched due to bad weather and poor visibility. On September 14 he flew again, his second mission of the war, but was jumped by enemy pursuit deep behind their lines and shot down. Before leaving on that mission, he left a letter to be given to his parents in the event of his death. "Do not hesitate or falter," he wrote, "until the world is once more safe for women and children, and 'carry on' is my last wish."

1Lt. Jack Mathis. The Medal of Honor is not lightly awarded. But even against that measure, the Mathis story looms large. Jack Mathis was a local boy, calling San Angelo and Sterling City home. Stationed at Goodfellow with his brother Mark, Jack reacted to the news of the attack on Pearl Harbor and became a bombardier, as did his brother. On a mission near Bremen, Germany, in March 1943, as Jack peered over his Norden bombsight, a flak burst near the nose of his B-17 blew him across the compartment and tore a gaping wound down his side. Dragging himself back to his bombsight, he found the target and released his bombs. The last word he spoke was "bombs," so a crewmate added "away," enabling the pilot to resume evasive action. In 1996, Goodfellow dedicated its new fitness center in his honor.

LT. COL. LEON ROBERT VANCE. This touching photograph of Medal of Honor recipient Bob Vance shows him standing in front of his B-24 Liberator "The Sharon D" holding his young daughter. Sixty years later, Sharon, the daughter, came to Goodfellow to speak at the dedication of the Vance Deployment Center, pictured below. Vance was one of a small group of officers who got the new pilot school at Goodfellow up and running in 1941, arriving in February and spending the next two years as commander of the 49th School Squadron. Deploying to England in 1944, his Liberator was severely damaged over France on a pre-D-Day mission. Thinking a crew member had been unable to bail out, Vance ditched his plane in the channel and was severely injured. Tragically, his flight home to recuperate was lost at sea.

Maj. Horace Carswell. The Vances and Carswells became close friends at Goodfellow. Short and powerful, "Stump" Carswell was an instructor pilot in Vance's squadron. Like Vance, he served a number of stateside assignments after Goodfellow before deploying overseas. Like Vance, his aircraft was the B-24 Liberator. Like Vance, he earned the Medal of Honor trying to save crew members unable to bail out of his stricken aircraft. And like Vance, regrettably, the medal would be presented to his fatherless child. For Carswell, though, the overseas posting was to China, where on a solo sea sweep at night, his plane was crippled by fire from a Japanese convoy, leading to his fatal attempt at a crash landing. The Carswell Field House was named in his honor, fittingly, on the day the deployment center was named for his dear friend Bob Vance.

Col. Bud Day. After serving as a World War II marine, George "Bud" Day earned a law degree before returning to duty in 1952, serving briefly as the Goodfellow operations officer before going off to fly jets on two tours in the Korean War. On August 26, 1967, while on an F-100 "Fast FAC" Misty mission over North Vietnam, Day was shot down, captured, and eventually imprisoned at the Hanoi Hilton until March 14, 1973. Colonel Day was awarded the Medal of Honor for personal bravery while a prisoner of war. His shadow box (above) shows his astounding record as the second most decorated military officer behind Gen. Douglas MacArthur. Below, Col. Thomas Geary, 17th Training Wing commander, stands with Day and his wife, Doris, at the dedication of Goodfellow's visiting officer quarters, May 7, 2010. (Above, courtesy of David Caughenbaugh.)

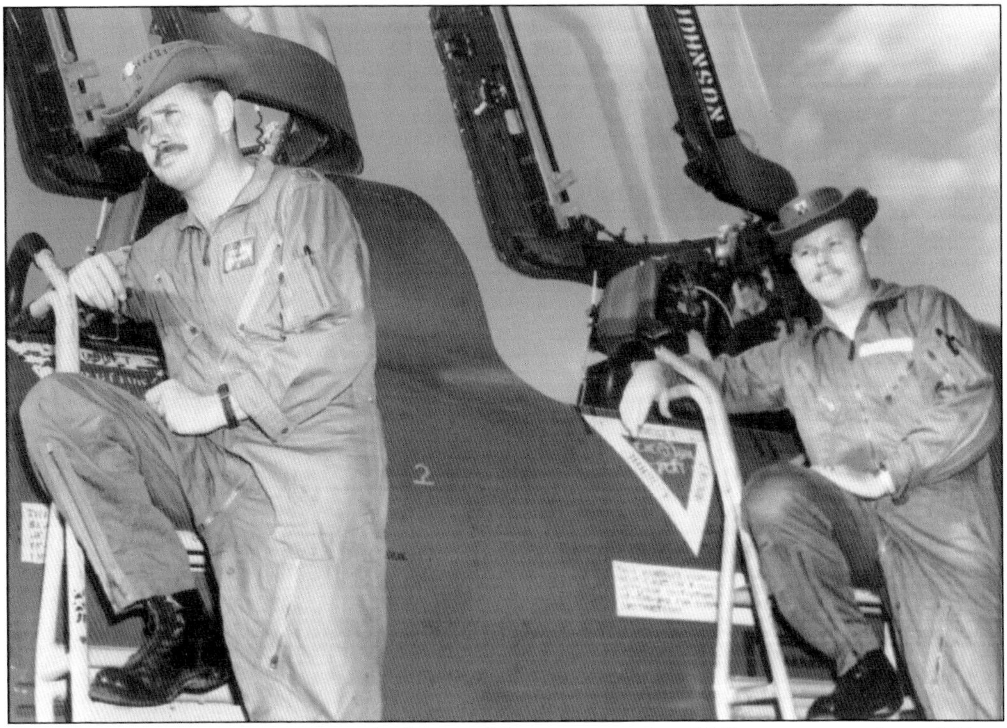

Col. Leo Thorsness. Thorsness had earned his wings at Goodfellow as a member of Class 54-G. Above, he and his backseater, Capt. Harold Johnson, pose pridefully perhaps in front of their Republic F-105F Thunderchief at Takhli Royal Thai Air Force Base, Thailand, in 1967. The team flew "Wild Weasel" missions to locate and destroy North Vietnamese surface-to-air missile sites. For one such mission, on April 19, 1967, he was awarded the Medal of Honor, but within days, and before he received it, he was shot down over North Vietnam during his 93rd mission of the war. Imprisoned at the Hanoi Hilton, he was released after nearly six years as part of Project Homecoming on March 4, 1973. Below, Colonel Geary stands with Thorsness and his wife, Gaylee, at the dedication of another of Goodfellow's visiting officer quarters on May 7, 2010.

Major Major. Few readers will have heard the name Randall C. Cassada. But Major Major, the delightful character from Joseph Heller's *Catch-22*, is far better known. Colonel Cassada served twice on Goodfellow as airbase commander. According to several sources, however, he was also the inspiration for the Henry Fonda lookalike Major Major while serving with Heller as a B-25 pilot during World War II.

Col. Norma E. Brown. Commissioned into the Women in the Air Force (WAF) program in 1951, Norma Brown began a stellar 32-year career in personnel and command assignments. Known as "Brownie" in her professional community, Elaine to her family, Norma to her military associates, and colonel (later, general) to so many airmen and officers, she thoroughly enjoyed every aspect of her Air Force life.

THE NORMA BROWN BUILDING. During 13 years with USAFSS, Colonel Brown championed the enlisted force, often working shifts, reveling at promotion and flight parties, and making tough, fair policy and command decisions. She was the first woman to command at the Air Force wing level, leading the 6940th Security Wing at Goodfellow during a difficult period of personnel reductions after the Vietnam War. She loved talking with young women considering the military as a career, counseling airmen just starting out, answering questions from junior officers seeking advice, and bantering with NCO Academy graduates while attending nearly every graduation. Air Training Command NCOs inducted her into the Order of the Sword in 1982, the year she retired as a major general. Goodfellow's new wing headquarters was named the Norma Brown Building in her honor on October 21, 2005.

TSgt. Ray Leftwich. Pictured with his wife, Betty, and children Raymond and Paula, Kansas native "Lefty" Leftwich served as a radio operator during World War II. Rejoining the USAF in 1954, he later served as an intelligence training NCO at Goodfellow before taking an assignment to Nha Trang AB, South Vietnam. He was killed in action on March 9, 1967. (Courtesy of Raymond J. Leftwich.)

Leftwich Hall Dedication. Leftwich is one of 36 airmen who lost their lives while assigned to EC-47 ARDF missions during the Vietnam War. Seventeen, including Leftwich, were intelligence specialists with the 6994th Security Squadron. Six, including Leftwich, have been memorialized on Goodfellow. Here, Betty Leftwich examines the plaque to be placed on the Leftwich Hall dormitory during the July 3, 1985, dedication. (Courtesy of Raymond J. Leftwich.)

Col. Charles Powell. If there were a face for the base, an image that immediately brought to mind Goodfellow and San Angelo and the bond between them, it would belong to Charlie Powell. At the zenith of a highly distinguished career that spanned four decades and included the Son Tây rescue mission, more than a dozen combat saves in Vietnam, and a term as Air University Chief of Staff, Colonel Powell arrived at Goodfellow to take command at a most difficult time, with the base slated for closure. When he retired four years later, following the longest tenure ever in command at the base, Goodfellow was no longer on the closure list, the base was postured to become a technical training center, a new PAVE PAWS radar site was planned for construction nearby, and Goodfellow had been named the site for the consolidation of all Air Force intelligence training. What better way to end this book than with a man who gave Goodfellow its new beginning?

Bibliography

Ashcroft, Bruce. *We Wanted Wings: A History of the Aviation Cadet Program*. AETC Office of History and Research, 2005.

Cameron, Rebecca Hancock. *Training to Fly: Military Flight Training, 1907–1945*. Washington, DC: Air Force History and Museums Program, 1999.

CAVU, 1941–1945, 17th Training Wing History Office collection.

Flight Time, 1942–1945, 17th Training Wing History Office collection.

Goodfellow Monitor, 1958–2018, 17th Training Wing HistoryOffice collection.

Hoover, Karl D. *Base Closure: Politics or National Defense Issue? Goodfellow Air Force Base, Texas, 1978–1981*. Randolph AFB: Air Training Command History and Research Office, 1989.

Manning, Thomas, et. al. *History of Air Education and Training Command, 1942–2002*. Randolph AFB: Air Education and Training Command Office of History and Research, 2005.

Marshall, Gabe. *The Aftermath, Oct. 29 and Beyond—USAFSS in the Cuban Missile Crisis*. Lackland AFB: Air Force ISR Agency History Office, December 12, 2012.

Mauer, Mauer, ed., *The U.S. Air Service in World War I*, 4 vols. Washington, DC: Office of Air Force History, 1979.

Myers, Harold P., et. al. *A Continuing Legacy: From USAFSS to 25th Air Force, 1948–2015*. San Antonio, TX: 25th Air Force History Office.

Nalty, Bernard C., ed. *Winged Shield, Winged Sword: A History of the United States Air Force*, 2 vols. Washington, DC: Air Force History and Museums Program, 1997.

Unit histories, Goodfellow Air Force Base, 1941–2017, 17th Training Wing History Office collection.

Schlossberg, George. *How Congress Cleared the Bases: A Legislative History of BRAC*. Journal of Defense Communities, Volume 1.

Tart, Larry. *Freedom through Vigilance*, 5 vols. West Conshohocken, PA: Infinity Publishing.

US Engineer Office, *Goodfellow Field, San Angelo, Texas, Completion Reports, Jobs A 41-1 and A 42-1*, 1942 and 1943, 17th Training Wing History Office collection.

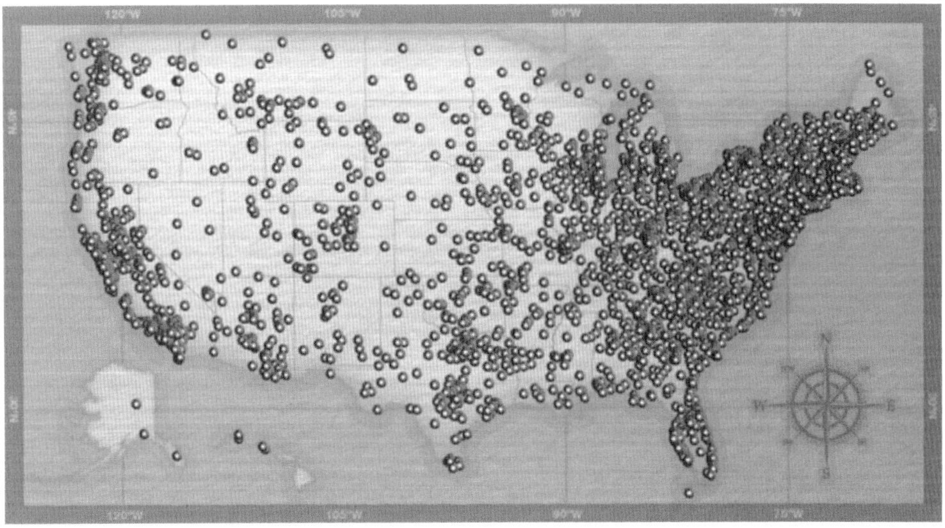

Consistent with our mission to preserve history on a local level, this book was printed in South Carolina on American-made paper and manufactured entirely in the United States. Products carrying the accredited Forest Stewardship Council (FSC) label are printed on 100 percent FSC-certified paper.

MADE IN THE USA